Conducting the Programmer Job Interview

The IT Manager Guide with Java, J2EE, C, C++, UNIX, PHP and Oracle interview questions

Janet Burleson

I dedicate this book to my husband Don, my one true love and best friend.

--- Janet Burleson

Conducting the Programmer Job Interview
The IT Manager Guide with Java, J2EE, C, C++, UNIX, PHP and Oracle interview questions

By Janet Burleson

Published by: Rampant TechPress, Kittrell, North Carolina, USA

Editors: John Lavender, Janet Burleson and Kelly Gay

Production Editor: Teri Wade

Production Manager: Linda Webb

Cover Design: Bryan Hoff

Illustrations: Mike Reed

Printing History:

May 2004 for First Edition

IT Job Interview Series: Book # 3

ISBN: 0-9745993-2-8

Library of Congress Control Number: 2004101889

Table of Contents

Using the Online Code Depot

Your purchase of this book provides you with complete access to the online code depot that contains the sample questions and answers.

All of the interview questions in this book are located at the following URL:

www.rampant.cc/job_prog.htm

All of the sample tests and questions in this book will be available for download, ready to use for your next interview.

If you need technical assistance in downloading or accessing the scripts, please contact Rampant TechPress at info@rampant.cc.

Get the Advanced Oracle Monitoring and Tuning Script Collection

The complete collection from Mike Ault, the world's best DBA.

Packed with 590 ready-to-use Oracle scripts, this is the definitive collection for every Oracle professional DBA.

It would take many years to develop these scripts from scratch, making this download the best value in the Oracle industry.

It's only $39.95 (less than 7 cents per script!)

To buy for immediate download, go to
www.rampant.cc/aultcode.htm

Conventions Used in this Book

It is critical for any technical publication to follow rigorous standards and employ consistent punctuation conventions to make the text easy to read.

However, this is not an easy task. Within computer programming technologies there are many varieties of notations that can confuse a reader. Some programming syntax, such as J2SE and J2SE SDK, use CAPITAL letters, while programming parameters and procedures have varying naming conventions in the programmer documentation.

It is also important to remember that many programmer commands are case sensitive, and will be left in their original executable form, and never altered with italics or capitalization. Hence, all Rampant TechPress books follow these conventions:

Source Code – Anything that might appear in a programmer program, including code snippets, keywords, method names, variables names, class names, and interface names will use a `monospaced font`.

New Terms – An *Italics font* will be used for all new terms, book titles and for emphasis.

Parameters and Placeholders – A *lowercase italics* font will be used to identify any command-line parameters or placeholders required by the user.

Commands and Programmer Programs – A `bold monospaced font` will be used to identify programmer binaries or command-line applications that will need to be typed by the user.

Products – All products that are known to the author are capitalized according to the vendor specifications (IBM, DBXray, Sun Microsystems, etc). All names known by Rampant TechPress to be trademark names appear in this text as initial caps. References to UNIX are always made in uppercase.

Acknowledgements

This type of highly technical reference book requires the dedicated efforts of many people. Even though I am the author, my work ends when I deliver the content. After each chapter is delivered, experienced copy editors polish the grammar and syntax. The finished work is then reviewed as page proofs and turned over to the production manager, who arranges the creation of the online code depot and manages the cover art, printing, distribution, and warehousing. In short, the author played a small role in the development of this book, and I need to thank and acknowledge everyone who helped bring this book to fruition:

John Lavender, for his expert operational management.

Teri Wade, for her hard work formatting the manuscript and producing the page proofs.

Linda Webb, for her production management, including the coordination of the cover art, page proofing, printing, and distribution.

Jeff Hunter, for providing much of the front-matter and questions.

Adam Haeder, for contributing the UNIX questions.

Don Burleson, the love of my life, for giving me the inspiration and assistance that I needed to complete this project.

Kelly Gay, for her expert page-proofing services.

With my sincere thanks,

Janet Burleson

Preface

After interviewing countless candidates for programmer-related positions, I am aware that it is getting harder to locate and retain qualified computer programmers. You must cull the best fit from hundreds of résumés. Success depends upon knowing exactly which skills you need and verifying that each candidate possesses acceptable levels of those skills.

That's where this book can be helpful. For both the new IT manager and the seasoned VP, the various levels within the computer programming position will be explained to illustrate screening and interview techniques.

Some common misconceptions about the computer programming position will be clarified and tips will be provided on how to successfully interview a candidate for this type of position.

Few IT managers, especially in smaller companies, have extensive formal training in interviewing and hiring techniques. In most instances the interviewers' primary full-time responsibilities lie elsewhere.

In many cases IT managers do not have a clear idea of the skills and personal characteristics their candidate should possess, or an effective process for screening potential employees. Yet nothing is more crucial to the success of the organization than doing everything possible to ensure that the selected candidate is the best fit for the available position.

This book will provide effective techniques for finding committed employees who are able to function at a high level on the job. By eliminating guesswork and rejecting the random hit-

or-miss approach that is based on the instincts of the interviewer and little else, the employer can hire confidently.

To help find, hire, and retain suitable computer programmers, background evaluation tips will be provided for identifying the best candidates.

For the technical interview, sample questions and answers are also provided. A non-technical evaluation section is provided to help determine whether the candidate's personality is a good match for the organization and whether the candidate will be able to integrate seamlessly with your shop's particular culture.

Of course, there is no magic formula for determining if a candidate can perform properly, and no single screening test to ensure that you will properly evaluate a candidate's ability. However, if the employer and candidate are properly prepared, then filling the position successfully becomes less of a risk.

It is my hope that this book will become an indispensable tool for identifying, interviewing, and hiring top-notch computer programmers.

IMPORTANT NOTE:

The intention of this work is not to provide a comprehensive technical exam, and the technical questions in this book and the code depot are only intended to be examples. The only way to accurately evaluate the technical skills of a job applicant is to employ the services of an experienced technical person to conduct an in-depth technical interview and skills assessment.

Also note that the expected answers from the questions are highly dependent upon the version of the product and the candidate's interpretation of the question.

We have tried to make the questions as version neutral as possible, but each new release of every product brings hundreds of changes and new features, and these example questions may not be appropriate for your version.

It is best to have an experienced technical person administer the technical interview questions presented in this book.

Programmer Evaluation

Introduction

One of the results of the surge in computer programming popularity is an ever-increasing demand for top-notch computer programmers and developers. As more companies continue to utilize programming for their businesses, the demand for skilled computer programmers increases. However, this mushrooming need for computer programmers has created a vastly disparate job pool. Job skills range from software engineers with PhDs in Information Systems from top U.S. universities with 20 years' experience, to semi-literate computer programming trainees with 90 days' or less experience.

The result of the explosive growth of the programming industry is the evolution of a two-tiered job market. Many top-rated universities teach programming as part of their undergraduate Computer Science or Information Technology curriculum and produce computer programmers for career tracks in large corporations.

At the same time, trade schools and community colleges educate hundreds of thousands of capable computer programmers and developers. No matter what the economic climate, large corporations historically actively recruit their entry-level talent for mission-critical systems development from prestigious university programs.

Written with the IT manager in mind, this book provides useful insight into the techniques commonly used to identify the characteristics that make a successful computer programmer job candidate.

Preparing the Programmer Job Offering

One of the points that bears repeating is that top-notch experienced computer programmers are hard to find and well compensated, while inexperienced computer programmers are easy to find and hire.

On the high end, computer programmers with over 10 years' IT programming experience and graduate degrees typically command salaries ranging from $78,000 to $101,000 per year, depending on geographical location and individual skill.

The first step in hiring a computer programmer is determining the skill set, and level of skill you require, and preparing an incentive package. If your IT environment is mission-critical, then a seasoned computer programmer with at least 5 years of experience is your safest choice. Candidates, however, with high skill levels and many years of experience often require incentives to abandon their present employment.

Preparing the Incentive Package

If you want a top-notch senior programming professional, you may be surprised to find them in short supply, even in a down job market. While every manager knows that salary alone cannot guarantee employee loyalty, there are a host of techniques used by IT management to attract and retain top-notch computer programmers.

Programmers like to use the latest hardware and software!

In addition to a competitive salary, some of the techniques used to entice potential computer programmers include:

Flex time - Burnout can be a real problem among computer programmers who must typically work evenings, weekends, and holidays to stay current with many demanding and sometimes conflicting project tasks. Many companies offer formal comp-time policies or institute a four-day workweek, allowing the computer programmer to work four, 10-hour days per week.

Telecommuting - Many computer programmers are allowed to work at home only visiting the office once per week for important face-to-face meetings.

Golden handcuffs - Because a high base salary does not always reduce attrition, many IT managers use yearly bonuses to retain employees. Golden handcuffs may take the form of a Management by Objective (MBO) structure, whereby the computer programmer receives a substantial annual bonus for meeting management expectations. Some companies implement golden handcuffs by paying the employee a huge signing bonus (often up to $50,000) and requiring the employee to return the bonus if he or she leaves the company in less than three years. However, don't be surprised to find that some competing companies will reimburse the computer programmer to repay a retention bonus.

Fancy job titles - Because computer programmers command high salaries, many are given honorary job titles other than simply Computer Programmer. These include Business Analyst, Programmer Analyst, Programmer Developer, and Systems Engineer. Other computer programmer titles include Vice President of Software Engineering, Chief Technologist, and the new job title (used by Bill Gates), Chief Software Architect.

Specialized training - Companies commonly reward computer programmers by sending them to conferences and training classes and an entire industry is built around these large educational events. For example, every year thousands of computer programmers gather for one week in San Francisco for the JavaOne^{SM} conference. Here, great minds in programming get together to network, learn and celebrate technology, innovation, community, and education.

Defining the Required Job Skills

A number of computer programmers mistakenly believe that the job of the computer programmer is purely technical. In reality, the computer programmer must be efficient and knowledgeable in all areas of IT because, in many cases, he or she has the ultimate responsibility for overall design, implementation, and user acceptance of the final system. Because computer programmers are heavily involved in all phases of the software development lifecycle, they must have excellent interpersonal and communication abilities as well as technical skills.

Remember, knowledge of programming is not enough. An understanding of operating systems and computer-science theory is imperative as well. That is why employers like to hire computer programmers who also have a background in computer science, information systems, or business administration.

It's also critical to remember that a programmer certification only tells employers that the job candidate successfully passed a certification test on the technical aspects of the programming language. In the real world, a programmer certification is just one of many criteria used to evaluate a computer programmer job candidate. Other criteria include the following:

Excellent Communication Skills - As one of the key stakeholders in any new systems development project, the computer programmer must possess exceptional communication skills. Effective communication skills not only include speaking but strong proficiencies in reading and writing as well.

In many application development shops, it is the responsibility of the programmer or developer to communicate technical and sometimes highly complex information to top-level management as well as other public groups. As the central technical guru, he or she must be able to explain concepts clearly in terms of the big picture. The audience may consist of all stakeholders including management, users, DBAs, and other programmers participating in strategic planning and architectural reviews.

Formal Education - Many employers require computer programmers to have a bachelor's degree in Computer Science or Information Systems. For advanced positions such as a Principle Software Architect or Enterprise Development Architect, many employers prefer a Master's degree in Computer Science or a Master's in Business Administration (MBA).

Real-World Experience - This requirement is the catch-22 for newbies who possess only a programmer certification. A common complaint among those who have programmer certification but no job experience is that they cannot get experience without a job, and they cannot get a job without experience. This is especially true in a tight job market.

Problem Solving Abilities - A successful candidate should also have the ability to translate raw concepts from vague design specs and paper-based storyboards, through prototypes, and all the way to a finished product. When analyzing problems in development, experienced computer programmers are able to recommend and implement effective solutions throughout all phases of development. They possess a deep-seated desire to develop innovative learning and teaching products and show profound capabilities for learning new topics. With excellent problem solving and organizational skills, a good candidate will possess the ability to evaluate information while making efficient architectural and design decisions.

Knowledge of Object-Oriented Design Theory - In addition to mastering the technical details required for the programmer certification exams, the successful computer programmer must have an understanding of object-oriented design methodologies. This includes intimate knowledge of object-oriented design theory, object-oriented application design, CRC methods, design patterns as well as object-oriented modeling with Unified Modeling Language (UML).

Basic IT Skills

Because the computer programmer is often called upon to participate in critical projects in the IT department, a broad background is often desirable. Much of this basic IT knowledge is taught in academic Computer Science and Information Technology programs. Non-computer programming job skills include:

System Analysis & Design - Many computer programmers must take an active role in analyzing and designing new application systems. Hence, knowledge of relational databases, data flow diagrams, CASE tools, entity-relation modeling, and design techniques enhance the computer programmer's scope of ability.

Database Design - Depending on the application being designed, many computer programming jobs require knowledge of some database theory, STAR schema design, and data modeling techniques.

Data Security Principles - An understanding of database security, including role-based security, is useful, especially for US Government positions.

Code Depot Username = reader, Password = nova

XML and Web Services - Knowledge of XML and Web Services (UDDI, SOAP, ebXML, WDSL) is essential when designing distributed enterprise systems.

Change Control Management - In many cases, the computer programmer will be responsible for utilizing version control and code sharing systems to ensure that changes to the production code base are properly coordinated. Knowledge of third-party change control tools, such as the UNIX Source Code Control System (SCCS), CVS, Oracle SCM, or Continuus is essential.

Now that we have an understanding of some of the required skills, let's talk about programmer certification. Certification can be used as one of several minimum employment requirements.

However, as interviewers frequently discover, certification provides no guarantee that a candidate has real programmer development expertise.

Characteristics of the Professional Programmer

Many application development shops have hundreds of technology workers. However, retention efforts are normally focused on seasoned computer programmers, whose knowledge of the company's application systems is not easily transferred to replacements.

In many development shops, the computer programmer may fill many roles. In addition to the traditional responsibilities found in software engineering, the computer programmer is often called upon to serve as a system architect, a database administrator, or a system administrator. He or she may also be asked to serve as an "informaticist" (a functional IT professional with an MS in computer science who is also trained in professional areas, such as medicine, business management, or accounting).

A first rate computer programmer might possess the following attributes:

Has earned at least one professional degree or certification - Having a degree such as MD, JD, MBA, MSEE, or CPA, in addition to an undergraduate degree, makes an employee a valuable asset, and one difficult to replace in the open job market.

Has graduated from a competitive university - Computer programmers must be self-starting and highly motivated to be effective. These qualities are often shared by those who've gained entrance into competitive universities with rigorous admission standards. These schools include most Ivy League schools, especially MIT, and universities with stellar reputations in Information Systems such as Purdue, the University of Texas, the University of California at Los Angeles, the University of San Diego, and the University of California at Berkeley.

Is trained in a special skill - Computer programmers with specialized, difficult-to-find training are often in high demand. Such programmers have skills in areas such as ERP Systems (Oracle 11i, SAP, BaaN), Relational Database Technologies (Oracle, MySQL, PostGress), and J2EE Platforms (Oracle9iAS, BEA WebLogic, IBM WebSphere).

Active in the programmer community - Many good computer programmers participate in local user groups, present techniques, and publish in many of the programming related periodicals such as Dr. Dobbs.

Is recognized as a programming expert - A sure sign of a top-notch computer programmer is someone who comes to the forefront of audiences by publishing a book, writing a magazine article, or appearing as a conference speaker.

Possesses irreplaceable knowledge of an institution's enterprise systems - If the employee serves in a mission-critical role such as Chief Architect or Principal Software Engineer, that employee's departure may create a vacuum in the Application Development Department.

Sample Job Sheet for a Senior Computer Programmer

Applicants for any computer programming job are expected to meet all the requirements in mission-critical areas, including education, experience, certification, writing credits, personal characteristics, and legal standing. Here is a sample computer programming job requirement sheet:

Sample Programmer Job Sheet

These are the minimum job requirements for the position of Senior Programmer Enterprise Developer. The HR department will pre-screen all candidates for the following job skills and experience.

Education

Persons should have a Bachelor's and a Master's Degree, preferably from a recognized technology institution. At a minimum, the candidate is expected to possess a four-year degree from a fully-accredited university in a discipline such as Computer Science, Software Engineering, or Engineering (electrical, mechanical, or chemical), or a BA or MBA in Information Systems (from an AACSB accredited university).

Work Experience

The candidate should have five or more years of programming experience in object-oriented programming, two or more years programming experience with the (insert language here), and three or more years experience programming in UNIX/Linux system environments.

Programmer Certification

The computer programming candidate must have earned a platform/language specific certification at some time in the last 10 years.

Publishing and Research

The candidate should show an active interest in publishing programming research by participating in user groups and publishing articles, books, and columns on the subject. These include:

Books. Submitting proposals for publication to programmer technical book publishers or any other recognized academic publication company.

Articles for academic journals. Publishing articles in academic journals such as the *Journal of the IEEE*, *Management Science*, *Journal of Management Information Systems* and the *Journal of Systems & Software*.

Conference papers. Writing papers and presenting at conferences such as Oracle World, JAOO, and Colorado Software Summit.

Articles in trade publications. Writing articles for a trade publications such as *Dr. Dobbs Journal*.

Personal Integrity

This position requires designing and coding mission-critical applications and accessing confidential data, so all candidates are required to sign a waiver to disclose personal information.

The candidate must have no history of acts of moral turpitude, drug use, dishonesty, lying, cheating, or theft.

USA Citizenship

We are unable to sponsor H1-B foreign consultants. Therefore, candidates must provide proof of US citizenship.

Additional Specialized Skills

The following specialized skills are desired:

- Bachelors or Masters Degree from a major university.

- Active US Secret, Top secret or Q-level security clearance.

- Working knowledge of Oracle9*i*AS Containers for J2EE (OC4J).

- Ability to use case design.

- Ability to work with human resource systems from Oracle11*i*, SAP, or PeopleSoft.

- Strong knowledge in UNIX scripting languages including KSH and BASH

Positions as a computer programmer have requirements that vary widely, and it is up to the IT manager to choose those qualities most suitable for the position.

Conclusion

This chapter has been concerned with identifying the job requirements of a skilled and experienced computer programming candidate and in preparing an incentive package. Next, let's take a look at how to evaluate the computer programmer for specific job skills.

Successful Programmer Qualities

Determining the quality of a successful candidate starts with evaluating the résumé. This is a critical part of the selection process. In a tight job market, it is not uncommon for HR and IT management to receive hundreds of résumés. It is important that they understand how to fairly and efficiently pre-screen applicants and only forward qualified individuals to the hiring manager for an interview. Let's start by looking at techniques for assessing the job history of a computer programmer.

A good computer programmer will demonstrate persistence!

Evaluating Employment History

Without question, a critical appraisal of a computer programmer's work history is the single most important factor in résumé screening. In most cases, candidates without a significant amount of work history will need to spend an excessive amount of time learning their jobs, while a higher-paid, experienced, ready to perform candidate may be a better overall value for the hiring company.

Not all programming experience is equal. Many demanding application development shops provide exceptional training and experience, while others provide only glancing exposure to the programmer environment.

When evaluating the work experience of a computer programmer candidate, the following factors should be considered:

Job role - Computer programming candidates who have held positions of responsibility in areas that require design and architecture decisions are often more qualified than those candidates for whom computer programming skills were a part-time duty.

Employer-sponsored programmer education - Within many large corporations, IT employees are encouraged and, in some cases, required to participate in annual training events to keep their skill sets current. One good indicator of how current an applicant's job skills are is how much on-the-job education is cited on his or her résumé. Employer-sponsored, yearly programmer training and participation in programmer groups and conferences are indications of a good background for a computer programmer.

Fraudulent Work History

In the soft market of the early twenty-first century, it is not uncommon for a desperate computer programmer to forge a work history with a defunct dot-com. The desperate applicant hopes that this fraud will not be detected. This phenomenon presents the IT manager with a unique challenge in verifying employment history with a company that no longer exists or contacting job references who, perhaps, cannot even speak English.

In many cases, the HR staff tends to discount résumés with employment and educational history that cannot be completely verified. Many departments, frustrated with confirming overseas employment histories, never forward these types of résumés to the IT manager.

Evaluating Personal Integrity

It is always a good idea to perform a background check, which is easily obtained via various national services. Many companies require that a candidate not have any criminal convictions, except minor traffic violations. In some cases, a routine background check can reveal arrests and acts of moral turpitude.

A computer programmer's ongoing responsibilities often include designing and coding mission-critical applications with confidential data. Therefore, some companies require that all applicants for computer programmer or developer positions be expected to demonstrate the highest degree of personal and moral integrity.

In addition, background checks that reveal a history of drug use, dishonesty, lying, cheating, or theft may be grounds for immediate rejection. In some companies, all applicants are expected to sign a waiver to disclose personal information and are asked to submit to a polygraph exam.

Evaluating Academic History

While formal education is not always a predictor of success as a computer programmer, there can be no doubt that job candidates with advanced degrees from respected universities possess both the intelligence and persistence needed to be a top-notch programmer and developer.

The Quality of Education

When evaluating the educational background of job candidates, it is important to remember that not all colleges are created equal. Many IT managers tend to select candidates from top tier colleges and universities because they rely on the universities to do the pre-screening for them.

For example, an IT professional who has been able to enroll in a top tier university clearly demonstrates high achievement, intelligence, and a very strong work ethic. At the other end of the spectrum, there are many IT candidates who have attended vocational schools, night schools, and non-accredited universities to receive bachelor's degrees in nontraditional study areas. In some cases, these IT professionals lack the necessary technical and communicational skills required to succeed in the IT industry.

The type of degree a candidate has attained is also a factor in how suitable he or she is for the position. For example, an ABS or MS in Computer Science generally requires the IT job candidate to have a very strong theoretical background in mathematics and physics. Those with formal degrees in computer science tend to gravitate toward software engineering and software development fields that require in-depth knowledge about lower-level components in computer systems.

On the other hand, BS and MBA degrees in Information Systems offered by accredited business colleges (accredited by the American Assembly of Collegiate Business Schools, AACSB) tend to strike a balance between IT programming skills and business skills. The information systems degree candidate will have a background in systems analysis and design, as well as familiarity with functional program development for specific business processes.

Unlike computer science majors, information systems majors will have a background in accounting, finance, marketing, economics, and other areas of business administration that equip them to solve business problems.

Many IT shops save time by letting universities pre-screen computer programmer candidates. For example, MIT carefully screens grades and achievement, and this allows companies to choose computer science professionals from MIT with increased confidence in the candidate's required skills.

The type of job to be filled may determine the academic history required. For example, a programmer developer/programmer position may not require a four-year degree, while a lead programmer analyst for a large corporation may require a Master's degree from a respected university.

Note: This section is based on the author's experience in evaluating computer programmers and the HR policies of large application development shops. This section is in no way meant to discredit those programmer job applicants without the benefit of a college education.

Rating College Education

Many shops have an HR professional evaluate education, while other IT managers take it upon themselves to evaluate the technical quality of the computer programmer candidate's formal education. Fortunately, sources for rating colleges and universities can be found online. Many large corporations require that the job candidate's degree must be from a university possessing a first-tier or second-tier rating by *US News & World Report's* "America's Best Colleges" or degrees from exceptional universities (as listed in *The Gourman Report*).

Of course, not all jobs as a computer programmer require a college degree. For lower-level programmer positions, the formal academic requirements are less stringent, but the lead programmer developer for a large corporation must possess high intelligence, superb communications skills, and the drive and persistence that is most commonly associated with someone who has taken the time to invest in a quality education.

College Major and Job Suitability

There is a great deal of debate about what academic majors, if any, are the best indicators of future success as a computer programmer. However, it is well documented that different majors attract students with varying abilities. The following list describes some indicators used in large corporations for assessing the relative value of different college majors:

Engineers - Engineers tend to make great computer programmers, especially those with degrees in Electrical Engineering (EE). An engineering curriculum teaches logical thinking, algorithm design, and data structure theory that makes it easy for the engineer to quickly learn programming concepts. However, while engineers have unimpeachable

---

technical skills, their oral and written communication skills are sometimes lacking. Therefore, IT managers should pay careful attention to communication skills when interviewing programmer applicants with engineering degrees.

Business Majors - Business majors make excellent computer programmers and analysts because of their training in finance, accounting, marketing, and other business processes. Many business schools also require matriculated students to take several courses in Information Technology. Of course, not all college business schools are equal. When evaluating a programming job seeker with a business major, screeners should ensure that the degree is from a business school accredited by the American Assembly of Collegiate Business Schools (AACSB). There are many tiers of business schools, offering vastly different levels of training.

Computer Science Majors - Computer scientists typically receive four years of extensive technical training, and are ideal candidates for the role of jobs requiring in-depth technical ability. However, like engineers, some computer scientists have less than desirable communications skills.

Music Majors - For many years, IBM recruited from the ranks of college musicians because hiring managers found that musicians possessed an ability in logical thinking that made them ideal candidates for IT skill training.

Math Majors - Math majors tend to possess excellent logical thinking skills and often possess a background in Computer Science. Like many quantitative majors, social and communications skills may be a concern.

Education Majors - Evaluation of education majors is extremely difficult because of the wide variation in quality between universities. Nationally, GRE test rankings by academic major show that education majors consistently rank in the lowest 25% of knowledge. Any applicant with an education major should be carefully screened for technical skills, and the college ranking checked in *US News & World Report's* "America's Best Colleges".

Some computer professionals are insecure about their vocabulary

International Degrees

A huge variation in quality exists among international degrees. Therefore, programmer candidates with international degrees should be carefully checked in *The Gourman Report of International Colleges and Universities*.

Some sub-standard overseas colleges have no entrance requirements and require little effort from the student. There has also been a rash of résumé falsifications of college degrees from overseas colleges. The fraudulent applicant is often relying on the human resource department's inability to successfully contact the overseas school to verify the applicant's degree.

In sum, international degrees should be carefully scrutinized. It is recommended that, where appropriate, foreign language professionals are hired to write the letters to request verification of the graduate's attendance, and to obtain and translate the college transcript.

Advanced Degrees and Programming Professionals

The percentage of computer programmers for large corporations possessing an advanced degree (Master's or Doctorate) is increasing. While an advanced degree shows dedication to a professional position, the quality of the degree is of paramount concern.

A higher ranking should be given to an on-site Master's degree from a respected university than to a night school or "non-traditional" graduate school. These non-traditional schools often have far lower acceptance standards for students and are far less academically demanding than the top US graduate programs.

The New Graduate

Regardless of the educational experience of the graduate, there will likely be little in the applicant's background that will prepare him/her for the real-world business environment. Computer curricula tend to emphasize theoretical issues of interest to academicians that may have little direct bearing on the needs of your shop.

The recent graduate may have grandiose visions of designing and maintaining whole software systems. They may be very adept at writing code from scratch, but will rarely be called upon to do this.

Recent College graduates can be immature.

Instead, your company will need someone who can work within the existing software system without crashing and burning the system. What's of major importance here is the ability to read OPC (Other People's Code). The candidate with the ability to slog through existing code and understand it is the candidate who will be able to add data and make changes in your production system without bringing operations to a grinding halt.

Moreover, the work that the new employee does on the software system will undoubtedly be modified and altered by others in the future, as new needs develop and hidden problem areas emerge. For this reason, a candidate who is able to show the technical interviewer that she has excellent documentation skills and habits can be much more of an asset to the company than someone who is not accustomed to submitting work that must be accessible to others. Several of the questions in Chapter 5 are useful in gauging these traits.

Personality of the Professional Programmer

What is more important to managers, technical knowledge or personality? Many times, managers concentrate too much on technical skill, while overlooking a candidate's personality.

In almost every core job function mentioned previously, the computer programmer's work comprises interacting with vendors, users, DBAs, managers, and even other developers. With that in mind, the following professional personality traits are, or ought to be, embodied by the successful computer programmer.

Some programmers have split personalities.

These traits are important for people in almost any profession, but they are particularly important for the computer programmer. Let it be said of the successful candidate that he or she is self-confident, curious, tenacious, polite, motivated, and a stickler for details.

For some programmers, everything is an emergency!

Self-confidence

Programming professionals that lack self-confidence, ask the manager's opinion on every decision no matter how large or small, and show no initiative, are not all-star material. This indecision may be acceptable for an entry-level computer programmer being supervised by a senior computer programmer, but the candidate should be expected to learn to depend on his or her own judgment for important decisions.

In interviews, questions must be asked about problems encountered and how the applicant would resolve the problems. Answers provided should reflect self-confidence.

A Curious Nature

Curiosity is a core trait of the computer programmer because the programmer platform is constantly changing, and it is sometimes difficult to find examples and documentation for those changes in the language. A computer programmer who is not curious is passive and reactive, while a curious computer programmer is proactive. The proactive computer programmer will install the latest version of the programmer platform and find enhancements that will make their code more efficient and easier to read, and in many cases, will improve performance.

Beware of computer programmers who don't take initiative.

The curious computer programmer invests personal money to stay current. In interviews with potential candidates, questions should be asked about the books and professional publications the candidate relies upon. Needless to say, answers indicating sole reliance on "the documentation set" are not an indication of professional curiosity.

Because curiosity is a requirement for a good computer programmer, another set of interview questions should involve the programmer APIs and the constant flow of new classes and packages provided in the programmer platform. A top-flight computer programmer is not lacking in awareness of the programmer APIs and of the basic classes and packages provided by the latest programmer specification.

A Tenacious Disposition

Like most disciplines in the IT industry, a computer programmer or developer requires bulldog-like tenacity for successful troubleshooting. The computer programmer should enjoy knuckling down on a problem and not giving up until an answer is found.

In the *comp.programming.threads* newsgroup, thousands of questions have been posted by computer programmers out in the field. Many times, the questions are about problems that would have been solved had the developer tenaciously pursued solving them rather than giving up.

Polite Manners

A computer programmer works closely with other people. Therefore, tact is required when dealing with managers, users, DBAs, and even other developers.

Some computer programmers have a reputation for poor manners!

But here's a fact of life for developers or programmers: Project managers, DBAs, and users will bring forth unreasonable requests and impossible deadlines. The computer programmer must cultivate interpersonal skills to respond to such requests without burning bridges. Ill-will is fostered outside the application development department by a rude programmer or developer. The computer programmer must be extra polite, beginning in the job interview.

Self-Motivating

Employers recognize and value self-starting employees. These are employees who require little in the way of supervision and constant spoon-feeding. Much more in the way of self-motivation is expected from the computer programmer than other IT professionals; primarily because they are the ones that must take charge of critical architecture and design decisions to produce a successful system. In addition, successful computer programmers foresee and prevent problems early in the system design, and seasoned professionals know what can cause trouble if they are ignored.

Motivation is a major factor in successful computer programming.

A self-motivated computer programmer will have a history of programming and debugging techniques that can be applied in making the most efficient use of his or her time during system development.

A self-aware programmer sees reality clearly.

In an interview, the successful computer programmer is able to respond to questions about programmer language fundamentals, application development, and application deployment by talking about the systems they designed and coded. Therefore, the interviewer can craft questions about specific techniques to identify candidates who have actually been involved in a project's critical design and architectural issues.

Attention to Detail

Being detail-oriented is perhaps the most important trait for a computer programmer. Like most IT professionals, computer programmers are often described as having an "anal" personality for their attention to detail, after Sigmund Freud's theory of anal-retentive personalities.

Attention to detail is critical for program debugging.

A good computer programmer should not have to be told to crosscheck details or to document quirks observed during the design or coding phases. A detail-oriented or systematic person is early for an appointment and brings a PDA or calendar to an interview. Questions asked by the detail-oriented person should reflect the research conducted about the potential new employer.

Conclusion

This chapter has been concerned with the specific criteria for evaluating work and academic history. Next, let's look at the roles of computer programmers and get more insights into the characteristics of a successful computer programmer.

Fluency in Klingon may indicate a personality disorder.

Roles for the Computer Programmer

Finding a well-rounded candidate

A good computer programming candidate is able to articulate a solid knowledge of techniques in all areas of programmer development, including coding and design, software configuration management, testing and debugging, use of the programmer API libraries, 3rd party code reuse, and code documentation using programmer documentation. In addition, a successful computer programmer in any organization must possess above-average communication skills.

Nit-picky computer programmers document everything!

Computer Programmer Job Roles

The job of a computer programmer means many things to many people. In many cases, the size of the employer will determine what is required from a computer programmer. In a small shop, their duties are much broader than in corporations with teams of programmers and developers dedicated to specific projects.

The functions of the computer programmer can also be determined by other factors, such as whether or not the employer is doing custom development. Are they utilizing third-party packages that require integration? Will the application be Web-based and if so, will it be part of an application framework that is ASCII compliant? The interviewee and the interviewer must be prepared to discuss and understand what is expected of the computer programmer and his or her role within the company hierarchy.

When a project begins that involves programmer application development, be assured that shortly after the kickoff, many talents within your IT department will be involved, including computer programming, developing, and analysis. Computer programmers will be involved from the start, interviewing end users, gathering business requirements, helping set expectations, and mulling over technical design issues. While coding remains the most crucial responsibility of the computer programmer, many application development shops include other functions as part of this job position.   Here are some common job duties for both computer programmers and developers:

Produce Specifications - Work with end users and project managers to write specifications that meet client requirements for applications. The programmer/developer will then work with clients and other consultants to program and code applications according to those specifications.

Determine User Requirements - Gather and work with requirements. This often involves Use Cases, UML diagrams, ERD diagrams, and other prototypes. The candidate should understand that the Use Case document is probably the most important of the documenting requirements. It contains the "stories" of how the user will eventually be utilizing the system. It is important that the candidate demonstrate past success in working with customers in documenting Use Cases and ensuring that they are clearly understood throughout the project life cycle.

Test Application Functionality - Work with clients and other team members to test an application's functionality, performance, and load according to specifications. Is the candidate able to demonstrate success in automating tests, performing unit tests, or using a testing framework like JUnit? The candidate should also have the ability to communicate those results to the proper stakeholders (project managers, executive sponsors, and so on).

Provide Technical Expertise - Provide technical advice and expertise to other technical team members within a project on system architecture, design, and technology alternatives.

Serve as Vendor and End-user Liaison - Serve as the official company representative and contact point for any programmer software/platform vendor(s) contacted for technical support. It is often incumbent upon the computer programmer to ensure compliance with programmer software vendor on license agreements for the company.

To sum up, a full-charge computer programmer candidate is knowledgeable in installation, project life cycle and methodology, software configuration management, programmer security, programmer application tuning, troubleshooting, vendor relations, and how to design and code application systems.

Let's drill-down and review the basic knowledge areas for the computer programmer candidate.

Application Tuning

Yet another one of those skill sets that is often more art than science is application tuning. It is almost always a requirement that an application not only be designed to solve a particular business problem, but be able to perform given a certain set of metrics. This often involves negotiating with end users and setting up user agreements and benchmarking requirements.

A successful programmer candidate should be able to bring forward and demonstrate tuning strategies they have used in the past that may or may not have worked. Was he or she ever called upon to investigate and resolve performance tuning issues at different levels of the application (i.e., the database, network, host operating system)?

Candidates should be prepared to discuss the pros and cons of Just-In-Time compilers, profiling tools, garbage collection, efficient use of looping, data structures, and algorithms, multithreading, and synchronization.

Troubleshooting

The flair for troubleshooting is a characteristic that is not common to all people. The art of troubleshooting requires an analytical and systematic approach, where the problem is laid out in discrete parts, and each is attacked in a methodical fashion until the problem can be resolved.

A dedicated computer programmer is always available!

Troubleshooting sometimes requires the computer programmer to admit he or she does not know something and must have the wherewithal to look for the answer. In responding to questions about troubleshooting, the computer programmer candidate should be prepared to discuss real-life experiences. The best examples are those illustrating a lot of thought and multiple troubleshooting steps.

Communication Skills

Great technical skills are needed by the computer programmer, but technical knowledge alone does not guarantee job success. As mentioned earlier, a computer programmer needs to be polite when dealing with team members, managers, vendors, and end users. Because a significant percentage of computer programmers' work requires interacting with others on multiple levels, they must be able to speak, think, and write clearly and concisely. A good computer programmer should strive to set the standard for quality oral and written communication skills.

An inventory of a computer programmer's communication skills starts with the professional résumé. Their résumé should be easy to read and reflect the candidate's publishing and speaking credits. Whether they were a keynote speaker at a national conference or merely presented a topic at a local user group, those experiences document the candidate's communication skills.

The interviewer should bring questions about job experiences that required the candidate to write documentation or procedures. It should be assumed that candidates with an advanced degree, such as a Master's or PhD, have well-developed writing skills, or they would not have reached that level of education. Candidates should be encouraged to bring to the interview their dissertations or other writing samples.

A successful computer programmer absolutely must possess strong verbal communication skills. The ability to listen is just as important as the ability to speak clearly. Their daily routine will include listening to complaints and requests, processing that information, and providing responses and instructions.

Conclusion

In sum, the computer programmer must have a well-rounded skill set, including more than just technical skills. Next, let's explore screening techniques for computer programmers and examine techniques and tools for verifying technical skill.

Appearances can be deceiving; you can't always spot a successful programmer.

Conducting the Programmer Job Interview

Initial Screening

CHAPTER 4

Preparation

Thorough preparation and attention to detail during the screening process can save significant amounts of money and resources as well as prevent potentially disastrous problems from ever occurring. Filling vacant positions is expensive, and a careful approach during the initial screening can reap tremendous dividends over time.

Be sure to screen for mental health issues!

In the opinion of many IT managers, an effective computer programmer should have plenty of significant real-world experience to supplement technical knowledge. It has become trendy in the past few years to create sub-categories of job roles, such as Development, Production and Production Support. However, in many large corporations, the computer programmer is the respected technical guru who participates in all phases of system development, from the initial system analysis to the final physical implementation. Hence, the computer programmer generally has significant experience in development and systems analysis.

Troubleshooting skills are essential for the computer programmer.

The High Cost of Attrition and Hiring Overhead

The IT industry suffers from one of the highest attrition rates of all professional jobs. This is due, in part, to the dynamic nature of technology.

An individual may find himself grossly underpaid and decide to market his skills within a relatively short period of time. Someone else may experience a lack of challenge in a job that he or she has successfully performed for some time.

For example, an IT job candidate might enter a shop that needs a great deal of work done, only to stabilize the environment to the point that they are bored most of the time. The IT manager must try to distinguish between the "job hopper" and the individual who is changing jobs solely because of a personal need for more challenging work.

The cost of hiring varies by position and by geographic location, but is rarely less than $10,000 per employee. Filling higher end positions, such as Senior Programmer/Enterprise Developer, can often exceed $50,000, as specialized headhunters are required to locate the candidate, and these headhunters commonly charge up to 50 percent of the candidate's first-year wages for a successful placement.

There are also the fixed costs of performing background checks and credit checks, as well as HR overhead incurred in checking the individual's transcripts and other résumé information.

Choosing Viable Candidates

While reviewing hundreds of applications for a single job, the IT manager must quickly weed-out "posers" and job candidates who do not know their own limitations.

To be efficient, the IT manager must quickly drill-down and identify the best three or four candidates to invite for an in-depth technical interview by an experienced computer programmer.

Shops that do not currently have a computer programmer on staff generally hire a programmer consultant for this task.

Computer programming consultants are commonly asked to help companies find the best computer programmers for a permanent position.

Later on in this chapter, some of the questions used when evaluating computer programming candidates for corporate clients are provided.

"Yes, I know C++, J2EE and two other programming words."

Dealing with IT Headhunters

When seeking to fill a top-level IT position such as senior computer programmer, programmer enterprise developer, or chief architect, it is not uncommon to employ IT headhunters.

These IT headhunters can charge up to 50 percent of the IT job's base salary in return for a successful placement.

However, the aggressive nature of IT headhunters often does a disservice to the IT candidate, and puts the IT manager in a tenuous position. For example, it is not uncommon for the IT manager to receive résumés from two different sources for the same candidate, each represented by different head hunting firms.

In cases like this, it is prudent to immediately remove that candidate from the prospective pool, in order to avoid the inevitable feuding between competing headhunter firms.

When dealing with headhunters, it's also important to get a guarantee that the IT employee will remain in the shop for a period of at least one year and to amortize the payments to the headhunter over that period. Those IT managers who fail to do this may find themselves spending up to $50,000 for a job candidate who quits within ninety days because he or she is not satisfied with their new job.

It's also important to remember to negotiate the rate with the headhunters. While they may typically command anywhere between 20 and 50 percent of the IT employee's first-year gross wages, these terms can often be negotiated prior to extending an offer to the IT candidate. In many cases, this works to the disadvantage of the IT candidate, especially when the headhunter refuses to negotiate the terms, thereby making another candidate more financially desirable for the position.

General Evaluation Criteria

Remember, all computer programmers are not created equal. They range from the entry-level computer programmer to a fully skilled, fire-breathing programmer enterprise architect with extensive credentials. What level of computer programmer does the company require? Consider what happens if such a fire-breathing computer programmer is employed in a position that requires only code maintenance of several legacy systems.

That individual will soon grow bored and find fertile application development projects elsewhere. On the other hand, hiring an entry-level computer programmer for a slot that requires tenacity, drive, initiative, and top-shelf troubleshooting skills is begging for disappointment.

Not all computer programmers have equal intelligence.

It is not easy to match the right candidate for a given job. Given the choice between someone who could write an ECommerce system from scratch (but lacked certain personality skills) and a technically inexperienced computer programmer who demonstrates the personality traits mentioned above, the less experienced candidate is frequently the best choice.

The typical entry-level computer programmer usually has a good-looking résumé that is full of projects and jobs involving programming.

However, the interviewer must subtract points if that work involved third-party Integrated Development Environments (IDEs) that were pre-installed and the programmer's main duties were simple code maintenance.

When the candidate can't answer in-depth questions concerning the fundamentals of the programmer language, the person should be considered to be a "programmer newbie" rather than a programmer-level candidate. Inexperienced programmers often believe their knowledge is more extensive than it really is. In other words they just aren't aware of what they don't know!

Networking skills may be desirable for a computer programmer.

A rule of thumb for hiring computer programmers is to avoid hiring an overqualified person who won't be happy in a job with minimal responsibilities. In a shop that utilizes a third-party Integrated Development Environment (IDE) and relies on pre-configured code generators, an entry-level computer programmer should be hired who can jump into gear whenever required to perform code maintenance.

On the other hand, if a high-powered computer programmer is needed, an inexperienced computer programmer should not be hired, unless that individual clearly demonstrates the motivation for high-end learning and the desire to become a full-fledged computer programmer.

Gleaning Demographics from the Candidate

With the strict privacy laws in the United States, the IT manager must be careful never to ask any questions that are inappropriate or illegal. For example, asking the marital status, the number and age of the children, or the age of the applicant himself may make the IT manager vulnerable to age and sex discrimination lawsuits. Hence, the savvy IT manager should learn to ask appropriate questions that reveal necessary information, while protecting the manager and the company from potential lawsuits.

An IT manager certainly does not want to discriminate against a job applicant, but the demographic aspects nevertheless factor strongly into a hiring decision. For example, the job applicant that has three children less than five years of age may not be happy in an IT position that requires long hours on evenings and weekends.

Don't wind-up in court over an offensive interview question!

Another forbidden consideration is the age of the applicant. If the hiring manager works for a company that guarantees retirement where age plus years of service equals 70, then hiring a 60-year-old candidate could expose the company to paying that candidate a lifetime pension for only a few years of service.

Mature computer programmers can add spice to the workplace!

Other important demographical information in our highly mobile society is the depth of connection the IT candidate has to the community. Those IT candidates who do not have extended family, close relatives, and long-term relationships in the community may be tempted to leave the position to seek more lucrative opportunities in other geographical areas.

Given that this information can be critical to the hiring decision and at the same time inappropriate to ask directly, the hiring manager may resort to asking somewhat ambiguous questions to get this information. For example, the manager may ask, "What do you do to relax"? This open-ended question will often prompt the candidate to talk about activities they engage in with their families and with the community. Unfortunately in certain situations a simple question such as this could be interpreted as a discrimitory practice. The savvy hiring manager will take care to avoid asking any questions that could be considered the least bit inappropriate. Participating in casual small talk with the applicant before or after the interview can also be viewed as a covert attempt to gather forbidden information. The hiring manager must take care to avoid forbidden topics while interacting with the candidate at any time.

The Selection Process

Generally, the selection of a computer programmer can be accomplished in the following phases:

- Initial screening of résumés by the HR department (keyword scan)

- Non-technical screening by the IT manager (telephone interview)

- In-depth technical assessment by a senior computer programmer

- On-site face-to-face interview (check demeanor, personality, and attitude)

- Background check (verify employment, education, certification)

- Written job offer

Résumé Evaluation

As mentioned earlier, it is not uncommon to receive hundreds of résumés for a particular programmer job position. The goal of the IT manager (or HR department) is to filter through this mountain of résumés and identify the most-qualified candidates for the job interview.

The HR department typically performs a quick filtering through a large stack of résumés to narrow the candidates down to a select few, which are in turn presented to the IT manager.

Some résumés may contain anomalies that can reduce the time required for screening. These anomalies are known as "red flags," and indicate that the job candidate might not be appropriate for the position. Such indicators can quickly weed out dozens of candidates, eliminating the need for a more detailed analysis of the résumé, saving company resources.

Résumé Red Flags

There are several important things to look at when scanning a stack of résumés. The following are a short list used by many IT managers:

Unconventional résumé formatting and font - Occasionally, you may see a nice résumé that is done in a professional font, but with elaborate graphics, sometimes even including photographs and illustrations. In extreme cases, résumés have been known to arrive printed on pink paper scented with expensive perfumes.

Too much information in the résumé - Another red flag is a résumé that tends to specify a great deal of non-technical information. For example, the job candidate may go into great detail about their love of certain sports, hobbies, or religious and social activities. In many cases, these résumés indicate an individual for whom the IT profession is not a great priority.

Puffing insignificant achievements - It is not uncommon for low-end IT positions to attract job candidates who will exaggerate the importance of trivial training. For example, an

IT job candidate may proudly list on her résumé that she attended classes on how to use Windows e-mail in the work environment. Of course, trivia within an otherwise nice résumé too often indicates a lack of real technical skill, and the job candidate may be making an effort to obfuscate that fact by simply listing anything that they can think of.

Gaps in employment time - It's important to understand that the technically competent IT professional is always in demand and rarely has any gaps in their employment history. Sometimes, IT professionals misrepresent their work chronology in their résumés. For example, if they are laid off and are job seeking for 90 days, they may not list that 90-day gap of unemployment in order to make themselves seem more attractive. Of course, the start and end dates of each term of employment must be carefully checked by the HR department, and any false indication of this should be grounds for immediate removal from the candidate pool.

Poor grammar and sentence structure - Because the IT industry tends to focus more on technical than verbal skills, you may often find candidates with exceptional technical skills, but whose poor writing ability is apparent on their résumés. Short, choppy sentences, incorrect use of verbs, and misspellings can give you a very good idea of the candidate's ability to communicate effectively via e-mail. Remember, the résumé is a carefully crafted and reviewed document. If you find errors in this, you're likely to hire a candidate who lacks adequate written communication skills.

Short employment periods — Within the IT industry, it is very rare to be dismissed from a position in less than six months. Even the incompetent IT worker is generally given 90 days before they're put on probation and another 90 days before they are dismissed from the job. Hence, an immediate red flag would be any IT employee whose résumé indicates that they've worked with an employer for less than six months.

"Yes, I was an NCAA Basketball All-star"
Some job candidates may lie!

Evaluating a Programmer's Training

Scanning résumés involves evaluating for two factors: work history and academic qualifications. Here are some criteria that have been used by major corporations for résumé screening.

Computer programming job candidates used to have only two sources for determining their knowledge: experience and/or programmer training classes. Experience speaks for itself and can be judged as to depth and level of experience. However, any training is only as good as what the candidate puts into the training. Candidates might either gain much or comparatively little from the experience of programming instruction, depending on whether they took their "will to learn" and curiosity with them to class.

In order to pass, a candidate will, in almost all cases, need to have had actual experience as a computer programmer and will need to have knowledge from multiple programmer references. The tests were developed by over a dozen highly skilled and experienced programmer developers and have been certified against hundreds of programmer candidates. While obtaining a programmer certification from these exams is no absolute guarantee that a candidate is fully qualified, it can be used as an acid test to separate the wheat from the chaff.

"I've been programming for 35 years."

Telephone Screening

After reviewing the available résumés, you will be in a position to select a pool of candidates for further telephone screening. The telephone interview is a useful tool for eliminating those candidates whose actual qualities may not quite match their glowing résumés, saving the time and expense of conducting on-site interviews.

The telephone interview may be either unscheduled or prearranged. In either case, the candidate will be less prepared than for the more formal on-site interview. It can quickly become apparent whether he or she is appropriate for the position.

The telephone is your best tool for pre-screening technical skills.

The un-scheduled telephone screening is an opportunity to discover how well the candidate thinks on his feet, and provides insight into his unrehearsed thoughts and feelings. It can also indicate how well the candidate is organized, since the person who must repeatedly search for basic necessary materials and documents at home is unlikely to demonstrate superior efficiency in the work environment.

The interviewer should cover all pertinent areas, with the goal of confirming the qualifications present in the résumé. The candidate should be well informed about those topics that the résumé indicates are areas of proficiency.

The telephone interview will also reveal a great deal about non-technical qualifications. Is the candidate personable and articulate? How well does he or she listen?

From information and impressions gathered from the telephone screening, the IT manager will be able to confidently select the best-qualified candidates for an in-depth technical interview.

Technical Pre-Testing

The job interview questions in this text are deliberately intended to be presented orally. These questions are designed to elicit answers that should indicate a high degree of experience and skill with a specific technology (or a lack of it). Many IT managers will require the job candidate to take an in-depth technical examination.

The technical examination may be given over the Internet, using job-testing sites such as Brain Bench, or they may be paper and pencil tests administered to the candidate before the start of a detailed job interview.

There are important legal ramifications for using these testing methods. Many job candidates who are not selected for an important position may challenge both the scope and validity of the test itself. These challenges have been applied even to nationally known aptitude tests such as the SAT and LSAT exams; IT exams, and language tests such as C++ and C#. These tests may be especially prone to challenge by the disgruntled applicant.

While it is important to do a complete check of all the technical abilities of the IT candidate, it is very important that a manager never cite the failure of one of these exams as the reason for removal from the applicant pool. This is a common technique used by IT managers when they find a particular candidate's knowledge of the field to be insufficient.

For example, in filling a highly competitive IT vacancy, very small things may make the difference between employment or not. In any case, when rejecting a candidate, the IT manager should generally cite something intangible, such as that the individual's job skills do not completely meet the requirements for the position; or a more nebulous answer, such as that the candidate's interpersonal skills will not mesh with the team environment. Remember, specific citation of failure of any tangible IT testing metric may open your company to challenges and lawsuits.

Developing Questions for Interviews

Interview questions should be diligently researched, and the expected answers listed prior to the interview. When open-ended questions are used, the interviewer should have the level of knowledge required to judge the correctness of the answers given by the candidate.

You cannot always identify drug users

The questions should be broken into categories and each should be assigned a point value based on either a scale, such as from 0–5, or according to difficulty. Technically competent personnel should review interview questions for accuracy and applicability.

At the conclusion of the interview, evaluation of technical ability should be based on the results derived using these point values.

In addition, "open-ended" questions should be included, such as "describe the most challenging problem you have solved to date," or "name one programming product that you have developed that you are most proud of". These open-ended questions are designed to allow the programmer job candidate to articulate and demonstrate communications skills.

The IT Candidate's Demeanor

During the face-to-face interview, the IT manager can glean a great deal about the personality of the individual simply by observing his or her body language and listening to the candidate speak. In many cases, the IT manager may assess the interview candidate on non-technical criteria, especially the behavior of the candidate when asked pointed questions. Some of these factors regarding demeanor include:

Eye Contact - IT candidates who are unwilling or unable to maintain eye contact with the interviewer may not possess the self confidence and interpersonal skills required to effectively communicate with end users and co-workers.

Fidgeting - IT candidates who are experiencing high anxiety during an interview may cross and uncross their legs, sit uncomfortably, or twiddle their hair while speaking with the IT manager. These involuntary signs of discomfort may indicate that the candidate does not function well in a stressful environment such as a result driven IT shop.

Diction - For those IT positions that require exceptional communication skills, such as working with the end-user community, you can get a very good idea of the abilities of the job candidates simply by listening to their responses. For example, careful IT professionals may demonstrate the "lawyer's pause" before answering the question. This pause, of about two seconds, often indicates that the job candidate is thinking carefully and formulating his response before speaking. You can also assess how articulate the job candidate is by the use of filler words such as "you know," inappropriate pauses, poor diction structure, poor choice of words, and a limited vocabulary.

"What is my long-term career goal?
Actually, I want to get your job."

Appropriate Appearance

A computer programmer job candidate who doesn't take the time to put the right foot forward by maintaining proper appearance probably doesn't have the wherewithal to perform adequately on the job.

Clean, appropriate clothing and proper grooming show that the candidate is willing to make the effort to please the employer. Candidates who are sloppy in appearance and mannerisms may bring those characteristics to the job and to their interactions with other members of the company.

Make sure your computer programmer understands proper dress codes.

Savvy computer programmer applicants will adopt the dress of the executive and banking industry for the interview. This attire generally includes:

- Crisp white shirt
- Conservative tie
- Dark suit
- Dark leather shoes
- Neat conservative hairstyle
- Minimal make-up

Proper job interview attire is important.

Conducting the Background Check

As we have repeatedly noted, a candidate's references must always be rigorously checked. Previous employers should be contacted, if possible, to learn about a candidate's past work history. Many people are good at interviewing, but won't necessarily function well in the job.

Because of the explosive growth of the IT industry, fraudulent résumés have become increasingly common. Job candidates have been known to fabricate their college education and the scope of their work experience, smooth over gaps in their employment history, and exaggerate their job skills.

In some cases, job skills may be exaggerated inadvertently, because the job candidate has only a brief exposure to a technology and does not understand their own limitations.

Therefore, it is very important for the HR department to perform a complete background check before forwarding any of these candidates for detailed interviews with the IT manager. These background checks may require the candidate's waiver signature for the release of all medical, criminal, and credit-related records.

The high rate of fraud found in job applications has spawned a new industry of private investigators that, for a fixed fee, will check national databases, revealing any criminal activity on the part of the job candidate, a history of bad credit, and other moral and demographic factors that may be relevant to their suitability for the position.

Conclusion

In sum, while the recession of 2002 has created a shakeout within the lower ranks of computer programmers, IT managers remain committed to retaining their top programmer talent, and those computer programmers with specialized skills are still in high demand.

In today's highly volatile work environment, the average computer programmer rarely stays with a single employer for a long period of time.

Competition remains extremely strong for those programmer superstars whose skill and background make them indispensable. While some attrition of computer programmers is inevitable, there are many techniques that savvy IT managers can use to retain their top talent.

At this point, you should be ready to invite the candidate for an on-site interview. Let's look at an approach to conducting a technical interview to access the candidate's level of technical programmer knowledge.

Preparing for the On-site Interview

Choosing the Right Questions

During the on-site interview, the computer programmer needs to be evaluated for both technical skills and non-technical personality traits that will indicate whether the candidate can be successful in the work environment.

Now it's your turn to ask the tough questions!

The specific areas that you choose to emphasize in the interview will depend on the nature of the position. A system's architect who coordinates the efforts of several people will need a different skill set than someone who primarily works only on code maintenance. Choose questions that will highlight the specific skills you need and look for past experiences that demonstrate those abilities.

An effective computer programmer must be able to wear many hats. He must have the discipline to manage multiple and many times conflicting tasks, the interpersonal skills to communicate with team members and project managers, and most importantly, the technical skills in programming.

This may include, but is not limited to, object-oriented programming techniques, accessing relational databases using JDBC, working with multiple Threads, GUI programming, and many other programmer language fundamentals.

Ask questions that demonstrate these abilities and look for experiences that show accomplishments in these areas.

Questions from the Candidate

Most books and articles neglect to discuss the questions that the candidate may ask the interviewer. This is unfortunate, because whether or not the candidate asks questions, the character of those questions can reveal a lot about his personality and suitability for the job.

After all, the serious candidate will be evaluating the company just as the potential employer is evaluating him. If he is able to ask intelligent questions that are intended to assess how well his particular abilities and goals will integrate with the job, he is actually doing part of your job for you.

A certain amount of nervousness is to be expected in the interview process, but the passive candidate who appears reluctant or unable to answer interview questions, as if under cross-examination, can only raise suspicions about the reasons for that reticence.

Contrast this person with the engaging candidate who doesn't answer so much as he conversationally responds, volunteering the pertinent information while interspersing his responses with questions of his own.

The candidate's questions should focus on the tasks and responsibilities he will encounter in performing the job. If the candidate takes the initiative in this way, facilitating the interview as you mutually explore whether the position is a good fit, chances are he will bring this same constructive approach to the work environment once you determine that he is, indeed, the best person for the job.

Beware of the candidate who only seems to be interested in his salary and the other perks that he will enjoy. There will be time to discuss money once you both decide that the alliance between you is promising.

The thrust of the interview should be on the requirements of the position and whether the candidate is equipped to meet them.

Telephone Pre-interview Questions

At some point in the process, you will be faced with a number of high-quality résumés in your file. Committing to an on-site interview costs time and money for both parties. It is therefore important to consider some pre-interview checking.

Performing a telephone interview to pre-screen geographically remote candidates can help in avoiding travel costs associated with an on-site interview. Also, you should ask to see their previous work or to contact a former employer. As long as you remain discrete, this is generally not going to be an issue.

While a quick technical check can be administered over the telephone, it is often performed by a certified programmer professional. Questions should be unambiguous, with a clear and accurate answer.

The interviewer should begin by apologizing for asking pointed technical questions before reading each question verbatim. If a candidate asks for clarification or says that he or she does not understand the question, the interviewer re-reads the question.

If the candidate fails to answer a question or answers incorrectly, the interviewer should respond "OK," and move immediately to the next question.

Conclusion

Remember, the only way to accurately evaluate the programmer skills of a job applicant is to employ the services of an experienced computer programmer and conduct an in-depth technical interview and skills assessment. For the best results, an experienced computer programmer should administer the interview questions presented in this book.

On-Site Interview Questions

Most Commonly Asked

The following job interview questions are almost universal and most job candidates can expect to discuss these issues during their interview.

1. What are your long-term career goals?

Expected answer:

> Here we are looking for evidence that the job candidate takes their career seriously and has developed a well-reasoned and realistic career plan.

> Remember, the interviewer will have their résumé in-hand, so they should never express a grandiose plan that is not reflected in their work and academic history.

> The best job candidate will have a realistic career goal, in-line with their education and circumstances. For example, it might be unrealistic to hear a 35 year-old high school drop-out with 4 small children at home talk about achieving an executive management position, while this might not be unrealistic for a 26 year-old MBA. The best answers might include:

> - I want to push myself to the limit, and I'm finishing Graduate School on evenings and weekends

> - I'm taking Internet-based training to improve my accounting skills and I hope to become a CPA someday.

- I'm always trying to improve myself and I don't mind working extra hours to learn a new job skill.

Answer: _____

_____

Comment: _____

2. I need somebody quickly. If you are selected, when could you start?

Expected answer:

This question should be asked with a sense of urgency, making the candidate feel as if they might not get the job unless they "screw" their existing employer by walking-out without notice.

This question will measure the candidate's sense of obligation. If the candidate is willing to walk-out of their existing job without notice, they will probably do the same to you someday.

Regardless of your implied sense of urgency, the employee should say that it would be unfair to just walk-out on their existing boss and that they feel obligated to give two-weeks notice.

Answer: _____

_____

Comment: _____

3. Can we contact your previous employers?

Expected answer:

This is a loaded question especially if they believe that the previous employer may not have a glowing recommendation for them.

In almost all large companies, the Human Resources person is directed only to confirm their job title and dates of employment, and nothing else, so they may be safe.

Remember, you may not need the candidate's permission to contact your previous employer, and this can be damaging if you can bypass the HR department and speak directly with their supervisor.

In smaller companies however, the manager-to-manager relationship may be fatal. For example, many managers know that they cannot sue for off-the-record comments and personal opinions.

For example, instead of saying "Joe did not perform his job well", the manager could simply say "I would not hire him," thereby making it impossible for them to pursue any litigation.

Answer: _____

_____

Comment: _____

4. Tell me about a time when you helped improve an employee's poor work performance?

Expected answer:

This open-ended question gives the candidate a chance to articulate their social and analytical skills.

Because the question deals with the possible hurt feelings of the poor performer, this is a great way to access the tact and finesse of the candidate. Top answers might include:

- I pointed-out the problem in an unemotional and non-threatening way, without attributing any blame to the worker. We then worked together to devise a solution to the performance problem.

- I was especially careful not to hurt their feelings but I was very clear that there was a deficiency that had to be corrected.

- I tried to work with the person to get to the root of the problem and made them feel safe that I was not going to report the poor performance to management.

Answer: _____

_____

Comment: _____

5. How would you compare your verbal skills to your writing skills?

Expected answer:

This question reveals the candidate's subjective judgment of their communications skills.

Of course, the candidate's résumé provides clues into their writing skills, and their oral skills can be inferred by participation on debating teams, college communications courses, and membership in Toastmasters.

Can the candidate comfortably discuss their own shortcomings, or are they the type of person who blames everything on others?

Most people will say that their verbal skills need the most work, but there is no correct answer to this question.

Instead, the purpose of this question is to see if the candidate is forthcoming about the deficiencies and willing to take corrective action.

Best answers might include accurate descriptions of their issues and insights into the proper corrective actions.

Answer: _____

_____

Comment: _____

6. Tell me about how you have handled an unsatisfied customer?

Expected answer:

This open-ended question gives you the change to show how you react under stress. Many candidates have very poor people skills, yet are so unaware of their own deficiencies that they sincerely believe that they are an empathetic person, when in reality they may be withdrawn and nerdish.

The best answer to this question should include references to identifying with the problem, an eagerness to act to correct the problem, and a sincere willingness to help.

- I emphasized with the end-user.

- I tried to get then satisfaction as quickly as possible.

- I was able to not take the issue personally and kept a professional and sympathetic demeanor.

Answer: _____

_____

Comment: _____

7. What is the description for your ideal job?

Expected answer:

This question is designed to allow the candidate to express their job goals and interest in tangible terms. The answer is not as important as their demeanor.

The best job applicants will not say what they think you want to hear and will feel free to express their personal values as they relate to the workplace.

The best answers to this question will be highly detailed with examples and illustrations of their ideal situation. Some of the best (and most honest) answers might include:

- I want to work in a stress-free environment where everybody has a team spirit and job goals are easily achievable.

- My ideal job would be working in a job where I had total responsibility for an important area so that I could work on my team-building skills.

- My ideal job would be for an employer that valued initiative and gave me the freedom to pursue profitable avenues of the business.

Answer: _____

_____

Comment: _____

8. What questions do you have?

Expected answer:

> This is the signal for the candidate to show you their insights into the operations of your company.
>
> The best answers should include references as to how they could maximize your company productivity and they should any avoid mention of company benefits and work environment.
>
> There is plenty of time to ask those types of questions after you have been offered the job.

Answer: _____

_____

Comment: _____

The next chapter will go over those questions that a good job candidate will ask and the following chapter will review inappropriate questions that a candidate should never ask at an initial interview.

What Candidates Always Ask

Two-way Street

A job interview is a two-way street and the candidate should always use the interview opportunity to ask question that may affect their propensity to accept the job offer.

A candidate should never ask questions simply for the sake of banter. Each question they ask should have personal value to them and they should only ask questions when they are invited to do-so by the interviewer. Remember, they are free to conduct their own interview after they have been offered the job!

Regardless of personal interest, there are some questions that every job applicant should ask. These questions show insight into the dynamics of employment and show that they are aware of the pitfalls of poor job opportunities.

1. What is the attrition (turnover) rate?

    This is the single most important question to ask at any job interview. Ideally, you want an employer who values the institutional knowledge of their employees and makes a sincere attempt to keep employees for long periods of time.

2. Why is this job open? Did someone quit?

    This can be a loaded question and you must answer honestly. If the candidate accepts the position and finds out that they are the latest in a string if dissatisfied employees, they may have a legal cause of action against your company for employment fraud.

3. What are my opportunities for advancement?

   This is a great question because it gives you a change to sell the company to a hot candidate. For those candidates who are unlikely to be extended an offer, this is not an important question.

4. Am I expected to work more than 40 hours per week? If so, how many extra hours per week?

   This is a very important question to ask because many employers want to hire young people on a fixed salary and then work them more than 60 hours each week.

5. What are the biggest challenges facing this department?

   This shows that the candidate has a genuine interest in the job and is concerned about their potential to find fulfilling work.

   You should provide an honest assessment of the current situation in your department, the areas of weakness and be very detailed about your expectations regarding the performance of the new employee.

6. What is your timeframe for making a decision?

   This is a legitimate question for every candidate, and one that you will likely hear from the top candidates. Again, an honest answer is appropriate.

Questions a Candidate Should Never Ask

CHAPTER 8

Best of the Worst

While asking questions is a sign of candidate interest, the candidate should be very careful not to make assumptions and ask inappropriate questions. For example, any savvy job candidate knows that pay and benefits are determined at the time of hire, and the interviewer will not be in a position to discuss specific remuneration items such as pay and vacation time.

They should never assume that they have the job, and should avoid questions that make it appear that they are more interested in compensation than providing value to your company.

Too many questions about company benefits are always in bad taste. They should know that if they are offered the job, they will have an opportunity to review the compensation and benefit packages, and the interview is not the right time to discuss these matters.

Some of the worst questions that I have heard from job candidates include these gems:

1. How often do I get paid?

    This is inappropriate because it indicates financial insecurity. As a general rule, lower wage un-salaried employees are paid weekly or bi-weekly while salaries employees are paid bi-weekly or monthly.

2. Do you offer tuition reimbursement?

It is never appropriate to discuss benefits and job details until the candidate has been offered the job. If this question comes up, you may say that the details of the compensation will be discussed in detail with the successful candidate.

3. Do you offer paid medical leave?

This is not only inappropriate but is considered a major red-flag by some hiring managers. Any job candidate who is concerned with such matters may be disguising a serious medical condition.

4. When would I start?

This question is extremely presumptuous and may indicate a lack of good judgment and tact. All savvy candidates understand that these issues can all be negotiated after an offer is extended.

5. How much paid vacation do I get?

Again, this is an inappropriate question because the amount of vacation is never known at this stage. You and the HR department have a huge amount of flexibility in offering vacation time, and this figure is often used as a bargaining chip after the job offer has been extended.

6. Is it OK if I take two weeks off before I start?

Again, this is a presumptuous question and one that is not appropriate for the initial on-site interview.

Any job candidate who would broach this type of question during an initial interview may have personal issues that may prevent them from performing up to expectations. Further, this candidate may be asking for additional time so that they can take your hiring offer letter to other prospective employers. For obvious reasons, this type of employee should be avoided.

Just for fun

If the interview is going poorly and the job candidate is certain that they would not take the job, they might want to have a bit of fun with you and deliberately ask some job-killer questions.

If the job candidate has self-confidence and wants to see how you react to absurd questions, you may have to handle questions like these.

Some of my favorites include:

1. Do you have an on-site Psychiatrist?

2. Does your company support my Constitutional right to keep and bear arms?

3. What does the company Horoscope predict for next year's earnings?

4. What is your long-term disability plan?

5. Is there a bar near the office?

6. How many warnings to you give before firing employees?

Next, let's discuss what happens after the job offer has been extended and the candidate evaluates you and the prospective work environment.

The Job Offer

Negotiations

Once the IT manager has chosen the first candidate, it is common to make an offer based on nationwide studies of the average salaries within the geographical area. For example, IT workers in expensive, professional, urban areas, such as New York City, will earn a great deal more than an IT professional with the same skills, working in a more economical suburban or rural area.

If you decide to make an offer to a candidate, it is a good idea to ask them the salary amount they have in mind. If the candidate is the first to mention a number, the company is placed in an advantageous negotiating position.

If the candidate indicates he or she will be satisfied with an amount that is lower than you were prepared to offer, then you have arrived at the ideal hiring scenario. You have a candidate that you have already decided is desirable for the position, and they will take less money than you had anticipated needing to pay.

On the other hand, if the candidate has an unreasonably high expectation given his skill level and the market in your area, he may have an unrealistic view of the current business environment.

This can indicate that either the candidate didn't do his homework or is simply the victim of wishful thinking. You might point out that the range for this position is somewhat lower than

---

he anticipates. You can then offer the amount you originally had in mind, and negotiate from there.

The knowledgeable IT manager will try to offer a candidate with an excellent set of IT skills a balance between the "going rate" and other intangible benefits, to make the job appealing. Other intangibles might include additional vacation time, flextime, telecommuting, and other perks designed to make the job more attractive to the candidates.

Of course, the savvy IT manager may deliberately reduce the size of the initial offer if he anticipates that the candidate may plan to negotiate for more.

A highly desirable IT candidate may be courted by multiple companies and will often respond to the job offer with a counter offer, citing other employers who are willing to pay more for the same skill set. When this happens, the IT manager may soon be faced with the dilemma of paying more than anticipated for the candidate, and may also question the candidate's motive for earning a high salary.

After the Job Offer

Once the candidate has secured a job offer, the interview process is only half completed. Now they must re-visit the interview process and determine of the job is right for them.

As we discussed, this is the proper time for the candidate to ask detailed questions about their start time, pay, benefits, vacation and work environment.

After the job offer is extended the candidate is in a position to negotiate all aspects of the offer. Of course, pay and benefits are normally hard to change, but adding another week to their vacation can commonly be achieved.

At this point the savvy job candidate will ask the tough questions to determine if the job will be suitable for them. Aside from the obvious issues of pay and benefits, the job candidate is most likely concerned with you, their new supervisor.

Evaluating you!

The candidate's working relationship with you is one of the most important aspects of their job and the single most important factor in their long-term happiness on the job.

We can usually categorize all employees, both managers and workers, into three broad personality areas:

- The Scientist Employee/Supervisor
- The Gung-Ho Employee/supervisor
- The Empathetic Employee/Supervisor

If your personality type is significantly different from the candidate, it does not necessarily mean that the candidate is a bad fit for the job. In many cases a variety of personality types mesh well as a team, off-setting the shortcomings of each type so as to work more successfully together.

However, dissatisfaction with management is one of the top reasons for employee attrition, so the job candidate's final interview before accepting the position should be used to ensure that you will be able to enter a productive and satisfying long-term working relationship with them.

Getting Along on the Job

By themselves, any of these three management personality types do an effective job. However, the problems begin when you have a personality conflict with the candidate.

Find employees with complementary personalities.

There is often conflict between supervisors and employees, and it is interesting to hear employees complain about the shortcomings of their boss. Here is a synopsis of some of the complaints that are commonly heard in the working environment:

Complaints from the Scientist programmer

The Scientist supervisor often enjoys working with an Empathetic supervisor, but has a real problem with the Gung-Ho supervisor.

The Scientist employee feels that the Gung-Ho supervisor is a "loose cannon" and cannot understand their impatience and disregard for detail. Secretly, the Scientist employee thinks that the Gung-Ho supervisor is dangerous, and cringes at their propensity to rush headfirst into everything without proper planning and preparation.

Complaints from the Gung-Ho programmer

The Gung-Ho programmer sometimes views the Empathetic supervisors as being lax and slow. They may also fault them for having what Mr. Gung-Ho considers skewed priorities (because in many cases the Empathetic supervisors may prioritize family and personal relationships ahead of work).

However, they have a much bigger problem with the Scientist supervisor, whom they see as rigid and overly cautious. Secretly, the Gung-Ho employee thinks that the Scientist supervisor should get moving and stop wasting time proving their theories.

Complaints from the Empathetic Programmer

Privately, the Empathetic programmer does not agree with the high dedication of the Scientist supervisor and the obsessive nature of the Gung-Ho supervisor, but they try to be understanding and are usually hesitant to voice any negative opinions that might hurt someone's feelings.

The Technical Interview

General Programming Job Interview Questions

IMPORTANT NOTE:

The intention of this section is not to provide a comprehensive technical exam, and the technical questions in this section and the code depot are only intended to be examples. The only way to accurately evaluate the technical skills of a job applicant is to employ the services of an experienced person and conduct an in-depth technical interview and skills assessment.

Also note that the expected answers from the questions are highly dependent upon the version of the product and the candidate's interpretation of the question.

We have tried to make the questions as version neutral as possible, but each new release of every product brings hundreds of changes and new features, and these example questions may not be appropriate for your version.

An experienced technical person should always administer the interview questions presented in this book.

1. What are the different types of loop structures?

   Skill Level: Low

   Expected answer:

   The correct answers are repeat-until, while and the FOR loop. The candidate should state that a FOR loop iterates a specific number of times, while the repeat-until and while structures iterate according to a variable or Boolean value.

Score: _____

Notes: _____

_____

2. What is the purpose of the GROUP BY statement in SQL?

Skill Level: Low

Expected answer:

The correct answer is that GROUP BY is required after the WHERE clause anytime an SQL statement performs aggregation (sum, min, max).

Score: _____

Notes: _____

_____

3. What is the default ordering of an ORDER BY clause in a SELECT statement?

Skill Level: Low

Expected answer: Ascending

Score: _____

Notes: _____

_____

4. You want to group the following set of select returns, what can you group on?

```
max(sum_of_cost), min(sum_of_cost), count(item_no), item_no
```

Skill Level: Intermediate

Expected answer:

The only column that can be grouped on is the "item_no" column, the rest have aggregate functions associated with them.

Score: _____

Notes: _____

_____

5. What is a Cartesian product?

Skill Level: Low

Expected answer:

A Cartesian product is the result of an unrestricted join of two or more tables. The result set of a three table Cartesian product will have x * y * z number of rows where x, y, z correspond to the number of rows in each table involved in the join. This occurs if there is not at least n-1 joins where n is the number of tables in a SELECT.

Score: _____

Notes: _____

_____

6. You are joining a local and a remote table, the network manager complains about the traffic involved, how can you reduce the network traffic?

Skill Level: High

Expected answer:

Push the processing of the remote data to the remote instance by using a view to pre-select the information for the join. This will result in only the data required for the join being sent across.

Score: _____

Notes: _____

_____

7. What is *explain plan* and how is it used?

Skill Level: Intermediate to High

Expected answer:

The EXPLAIN PLAN is a tool to tune SQL statements. To use it you must have an *explain_table* generated in the user you are running the explain plan for. This is created using the *utlxplan.sql* script. Once the explain plan table exists, you run the explain plan command giving as its argument the SQL statement to be explained. The *explain_plan* table is then queried to see the execution plan of the statement. Explain plans can also be run using TKPROF.

Score: _____

Notes: _____

_____

Section average score: _____

Skill Level: _____

Java and J2EE Versions

Several of the expected answers from these questions may be highly dependent upon the version of Java and the J2EE specification. While we have made every effort to make the questions as version neutral as possible, each release of the J2EE specification brings many changes and new features, and these example questions may not be appropriate for your version of Java/J2EE implementation. As a reference when determining whether behavior and syntax is correct, we use Sun's J2EE 1.3 platform specification.

Qualifications

1. Do you have any Certifications? (i.e. Java Programmer/Developer, Cisco, Microsoft, Oracle)

   Answer: _____

   Comment: _____

   _____

2. What relational database systems are you most familiar with? (Oracle, SQL Server, MySQL, Postgres, etc.)

   Answer: _____

   Comment: _____

   _____

3. What J2EE Application Servers are you most familiar with? (Oracle9iAS, OC4J, BEA WebLogic Server, IBM WebSphere, JBoss, etc.)

   Answer: _____

   Comment: _____

   _____

4. Which Java Development IDE are you most comfortable with? (JBuilder, IntelliJ IDEA, JDeveloper, plain 'ol Emacs, etc.)

Answer: _____

Comment: _____

_____

5. Which version control systems have you used in the past? (CVS, Oracle Software Configuration Management, Continuus, ClearCase, etc.)

Answer: _____

Comment: _____

_____

6. Highest level of education?

Most candidates in this field require a college education, preferably a BS in computer science, computer information technology or related engineering field.

Answer: _____

Comment: _____

_____

Section average score: _____

Skill Level: _____

Java Interview Questions

1. How many public classes are permitted within a single Java class file?

   Skill Level: Low

   Expected answer:

   You can only define one public class within a single Java class file.

   Score: _____

   Notes: _____

   _____

2. How many package statements (declarations) are allowed in a Java source file?

   Skill Level: Low

   Expected answer: Only one.

   Score: _____

   Notes: _____

   _____

3. Is it necessary to have a package statement in a Java source file?

   Skill Level: Low

   Expected answer: No.

   Score: _____

   Notes: _____

4. In a Java source file, which statement needs to come first, import or package?

Skill Level: Low

Expected answer:

The package statement must come before any import statements.

Score: _____

Notes: _____

_____

5. If all three statement elements of a Java source file are included (imports, classes, packages), in which order must they appear?

Skill Level: Low

Expected answer:

Package declaration, imports, and then all classes.

Score: _____

Notes: _____

_____

6. Consider a program that imports a large number of classes. Is there any performance degradation from importing many classes at runtime?

Skill Level: Low

Expected answer:

No. The import statements only provide the compiler with class name abbreviations and have no performance impact at runtime.

Score: _____

Notes: _____

_____

7. What is the command-line utility used to compile Java source code into bytecode?

Skill Level: Low

Expected answer:

The command-line utility is `javac`.

Score: _____

Notes: _____

_____

8. What is the name of the method the JVM uses as the normal entry point for a Java application? What is its signature?

Skill Level: Low

Expected answer:

The name of the method is main(). The signature for main() is:

```
public static void main(String[] args)
```

Score: _____

Notes: _____

_____

9. Is it a requirement that the `main()` method be declared as static? Explain why or why not?

Skill Level: Low

Expected answer:

Yes, it is a requirement that the `main()` method be declared static. This is necessary so it can be invoked without having to construct an instance of the corresponding class.

Score: _____

Notes: _____

_____

10. What are the four signed integral data types in Java? What are their sizes and range of values?

Skill Level: Low

Expected answer:

Data Type	Size	Minimum	Maximum
Byte	8 bits	-2^7	$-2^7 - 1$
Short	16 bits	-2^{15}	$-2^{15} - 1$
Int	32 bits	-2^{31}	$-2^{31} - 1$
Long	64 bits	-2^{63}	$-2^{63} - 1$

Score: _____

Notes: _____

_____

11. Within your Java application, you catch all exceptions and want to know the exact circumstances under which they occurred. Which method would you use from the throw able class to obtain a complete stack trace?

Skill Level: Low

Expected answer:

You can get a stack trace from any exception object with the `printStackTrace()` method in the throw able class.

Score: _____

Notes: _____

_____

12. What is the difference between System.out.println() and System.out.print()?

Skill Level: Low

Expected answer:

The println() method is used to display a line of text that ends with a newline character. The newline character causes the next line of text to begin displaying at the leftmost edge of the next line, similar to the carriage return key on a manual typewriter. The print() method, on the other hand, does not add the newline character to the end of the line. This allows you to use several print() statements to display information on the same line.

Score: _____

Notes: _____

_____

13. When creating a `string` object, is it necessary to use the `new` operator?

Skill Level: Low

Expected answer:

No. Java does not require you to use the new operator when constructing a new `String` object. In fact, it is more efficient than explicitly calling the constructor.

Score: _____

Notes: _____

_____

14. What is the value at which a String is automatically initialized?

Skill Level: Low

Expected answer: null.

Score: _____

Notes: _____

_____

15. How do you make a variable a constant?

Skill Level: Low

Expected answer:

Declare the variable using the final keyword.

Score: _____

Notes: _____

_____

16. What does putting the + operator between two strings do?

Skill Level: Low

Expected answer:

It concatenates the two strings together.

Score: _____

Notes: _____

_____

17. What characters can be legally used as the first character of a Java identifier?

Skill Level: Low

Expected answer:

Any letter, the dollar sign ($), or an underscore.

Score: _____

Notes: _____

_____

18. What statement would you use to convert the String `str1` to an integer named `int1`?

Skill Level: Low

Expected answer:

```
int int1 = Integer.parseInt(str1);
```

Score: _____

Notes: _____

_____

19. What statement would you use to convert the String `str1` to a byte named `byte1`?

Skill Level: Low

Expected answer:

```
byte byte1 = Byte.parseByte(str1);
```

Score: _____

Notes: _____

_____

20. What statement would you use to convert the String str1 to a long named long1?

Skill Level: Low

Expected answer:

```
long long1 = Long.parseLong(str1);
```

Score: _____

Notes: _____

_____

Section average score: _____

Skill Level: _____

Java Tuning Interview Questions

1. What is the Web address (URL) where you can download Sun's official Java Software Development Kit (SDK) J2SE?

   Skill Level: Low

   Expected answer:

   The URL is http://java.sun.com.

   Score: _____

   Notes: _____

   _____

2. Using Sun's Java 2 SDK, how do you check which version of the SDK you are using?

   Skill Level: Low

   Expected answer:

   You can check the version by using java –version.

   Score: _____

   Notes: _____

   _____

3. After installing the Java 2 SDK bundle, what are the most important environment variables that should be set?

   Skill Level: Low

   Expected answer:

   - **JAVA_HOME** – Points to the directory where you installed the Java SDK For example, JAVA_HOME=c:\j2sdk1.4.1_01

- **PATH** – Should contain the bin directory of your Java SDK. For example, PATH=%PATH%;%JAVA_HOME%/bin
- **CLASSPATH** – Should contain the directories and Java archives where the JVM will look for Java class files to load.

Score: _____

Notes: _____

_____

4. What is the environment variable CLASSPATH used for?

Skill Level: Intermediate

Expected answer:

This is an environment variable that can be set to contain the directories and archive used by the Java interpreter and the Java compiler when searching for packages and classes on the local machine.

Keep in mind that the CLASSPATH environment variable can contain directories and/or java class archive files (JAR and ZIP files).

Score: _____

Notes: _____

_____

5. If you do not set CLASSPATH, what value will be used by the JVM to locate and load Java class files by default?

Skill Level: Intermediate

Expected answer:

Only the current directory, "." is included. Ensure that if you do set the CLASSPATH path, you will need to explicitly include the current directory (".") if you want it in the CLASSPATH.

Score: _____

Notes: _____

_____

6. If the CLASSPATH environment variable is set and the -classpath option is used for the JRE, which one takes precedence?

Skill Level: Intermediate

Expected answer:

The -classpath option takes precedence over the CLASSPATH environment variable.

Score: _____

Notes: _____

_____

7. Sun's JDK includes a minimal profiler. What command-line option is used with the Java executable to invoke this profiler with Sun's JDK 1.2 or later version?

Skill Level: Low

Expected answer:

Using Sun's JDK 1.2 or later, use the Java executable with the -Xrunhprof option. (Using versions of the JDK earlier than 1.2, the command-line option is -prof.)

Score: _____

Notes: _____

_____

8. A common mistake programmers make is to perform "premature optimization" – trying to optimize code during code development. Why is it a bad idea?

Skill Level: Low

Expected answer:

The rule here is to simply develop code to work — make it correct and get it finished. Optimization is something that should be performed after development and only if there are known bottlenecks. It is easy to use tools to measure for bottlenecks. During development, it is hard to know where the bottlenecks will exist, if at all, in your code. Many developers and programmers waste unnecessary time during development trying to optimize code that will not be perceived by the end user. In many cases, the code that you develop will be fast enough.

Score: _____

Notes: _____

_____

9. What methods can you call in Java to encourage or suggest to the *garbage collector* that it reclaim memory?

Skill Level: Low

Expected answer:

There are two methods that can send a request to the garbage collector asking it to reclaim memory: java.lang.System.gc()   or java.lang.Runtime.getRuntime().gc(). The accepted convention is to invoke System.gc(), which is equivalent to Runtime.getRuntime().gc().

Score: _____

Notes: _____

_____

10. What is the command-line option with Sun's SDK that can be used to print out messages by the interpreter each time a garbage collection is performed?

Skill Level: Intermediate

Expected answer: The option is –verbosegc.

Score: _____

Notes: _____

_____

11. When tuning an application, you should monitor and determine if the application is limiting any of the three major computer resources. What are these three computer resources?

Skill Level: Intermediate

Expected answer:

- CPU availability
- System (RAM) memory
- I/O (Disk, network, etc)

Score: _____

Notes: _____

_____

12. When using the default profiler packaged with Sun's JDK 1.2 (or later), what is the default name of the results file that contains the profile data?

Skill Level: Intermediate

Expected answer:

With Sun's JDK 1.2 or later, the default file name is java.hprof.txt. (If versions of the JDK earlier than 1.2 are used, the default file name is java.prof.)

Score: _____

Notes: _____

_____

13. When using the default profiler packaged with Sun's JDK 1.2 (or later), is it possible to specify the name of the results file that will contain the profile data? If so, what does the command-line option look like?

Skill Level: Intermediate

Expected answer:

Yes, it is possible. The option would look like -Xrunhprof:file=*filename*. (Using versions of the JDK earlier than 1.2, the option would like -prof:filename.)

Score: _____

Notes: _____

_____

14. What is a Just-In-Time compiler and what are the benefits to using it?

Skill Level*: Intermediate

Expected answer*:

When using the JVM, the bytecode must be processed and interpreted one instruction at a time. A Just-In-Time (JIT) compiler can take Java bytecode and recompile it for a particular system platform. Using JIT will often enable the Java program to run faster.

Score: _____

Notes: _____

_____

15. What is the difference between the StringBuffer class and the String class?

Skill Level*: Intermediate

Expected answer*:

Both classes support the use of storing and manipulating strings — character data consisting of more than one character. Both classes contain similar methods for manipulating Strings and converting them to other variables.

A String object is immutable, which means you cannot change it. In a Java program, you may update a String object, but this will cause excessive computing cycles since behind the scenes, Java is creating a new String object to hold the new value. String concatenation via the +operator is one of the most convenient things to do in Java, but as you can see, is also one of the most expensive in terms of memory and performance.

The StringBuffer class provides for strings that can be modified. The StringBuffer class will grow and shrink to match the size of the file. You should use String buffers when you know that the value of the character data will change. This can occur in an application when you are constructing character data dynamically. Take for example, reading text data from a file or values from a database query.

Score: _____

Notes: _____

_____

16. What method in the StringBuffer class can be used to append character data to the end of the current data already within the StringBuffer object?

Skill Level: Low

Expected answer:

The append (String str) method can be used.

Score: _____

Notes: _____

_____

17. How would you return the content of a StringBuffer object into a `string` object?

Skill Level: Low

Expected answer:

Use the toString (String str) method of StringBuffer to return its contents to a String object.

Score: _____

Notes: _____

_____

18. Consider the following code snippet:

```
int x = 8;
int y = x/4;
```

Using bit-wise arithmetic, could you replace the operation in the second line with a faster and more efficient operation without changing the meaning of the statement?

Skill Level: High

Expected answer:

Yes, simply perform two right shifts of the x value:

```
int y = x >> 2;
```

Each right shift by one is equivalent to dividing by 2. In this example, 22 = 4; so you should perform two right shifts.

Score: _____

Notes: _____

_____

19. Consider the following code snippet:

```
int x = 4;
int y = x * 8;
```

Using bit-wise arithmetic, could you replace the operation in the second line with a faster and more efficient operation without changing the meaning of the statement?

Skill Level: High

Expected answer:

Yes, simply perform three left shifts of the x value:

```
int y = x << 3;
```

Each left shift by one is equivalent to multiplying by 2. In this example, $2^3 = 8$, so you should perform 3 left shifts.

Score: _____

Notes: _____

_____

20. Consider the following code snippet:

```
for (int i = 0; i < j.length; i++) {
j[i] = k * Math.sqrt(z);
}
```

Can you see any improvements that can be made to increase the efficiency of this code?

Skill Level: High

Expected answer:

As you can see in the previous loop, the elements of the array are being assigned the same value with each iteration. Not only is it the same value each time, it is being calculated each time, producing the same results. Since the calculation produces the same value each time, you should simply move the calculation out of the loop, calculating it only once. Then, you should assign it to a variable and use the variable in the loop as follows:

```
double z1 = k * Math.sqrt(z);
for (int i = 0; i < j.length; i++) {
j[i] = z1;
}
```

Score: _____

Notes: _____

_____

Section average score: _____

Skill Level: _____

J2EE Telephone Pre-interview Questions

At some point in the process, you will be faced with a number of high quality resumes in your file. Committing to an on-site interview costs time and money for both parties. It is therefore important to consider some pre-interview checking. Performing a telephone interview to pre-screen geographically remote candidates can help in avoiding travel costs associated with an on-site interview. Also, ask to see their previous work or contact a former employer. As long as you remain discrete this is generally not going to be an issue.

The following 10 questions should help in determining the technical skill set of any potential J2EE candidate. The questions are simple enough that any qualified J2EE professional should be able to answer them immediately from memory. If a candidate has a hard time with these questions, they may not be appropriate for a full time position as a J2EE Developer or Architect.

1. When working with a *Web application*, what is the filename of the deployment descriptor and where should be it located?

   Skill Level: Low

   Expected answer:

   > The name of the deployment descriptor for web applications is named web.xml and is typically located in the (web-app-root)/WEB-INF/web.xml.

   Score: _____

   Notes: _____

   _____

---

2. What is the name of the XML root element within the Web deployment descriptor file; web.xml?

Skill Level: Low

Expected answer:

The name of the XML root element is <web-app>.

Score: _____

Notes: _____

_____

3. What are the two J2EE Web-based technologies that support dynamic content generation of web pages in a portable and cross-platform manner?

Skill Level: Low

Expected answer:

JavaServer Pages (JSP) and Servlets.

Score: _____

Notes: _____

_____

4. You have a client application that needs to lookup the home interface of an enterprise bean. Which class and method is used to lookup the bean?

Skill Level: Low

Expected answer:

The application would need to use the lookup() method of the InitialContext class, found in the JNDI package. In order to access an enterprise bean, the application will use the JNDI package to obtain a directory connection to a beans container. Once the connection is established, a new InitialContext object is created. The lookup() method of the InitialContext object is then used to look up the bean. The lookup() method will return a reference to the home object of the bean.

Score: _____

Notes: _____

_____

5. What are the two ways in which an *entity bean* can persist enterprise data?

Skill Level: Low

Expected answer:

An entity can use either container-managed persistence (CMP) or bean-managed persistence. With CMP, the EJB container is responsible for handling the implementation of code (SQL) necessary to insert, read, and update an object in a data source. With BMP, the application developer needs to create the implementation code for the insert, read, and update of an object.

Score: _____

Notes: _____

_____

6. You have an application that uses Java objects exclusively. Which distributed technology should you consider for communication; RMI or CORBA? Why?

Skill Level: Low

Expected answer:

If you have an application that only contains Java objects, it would be appropriate to use RMI. The RMI technology is built right into the Java language as a means of allowing objects to communicate with other objects that are running on JVMs on remote machine within the network. Using CORBA technology, objects that are exported with CORBA can be accessed by clients implemented in any language (C, Perl, etc) with an IDL binding. Although CORBA is more extensive than RMI, RMI is more straightforward to use since it only used Java objects.

Score: _____

Notes: _____

_____

7. You are about the write a *Session Bean*. What are the three types of component (classes and interfaces) that are needed to write a Session Bean?

Skill Level: Low

Expected answer:

To write a session bean, you will need to create the following:

- Home Interface
- Remote Interface
- The actual bean class which implements the SessionBean Interface

Score: _____

Notes: _____

_____

8. Suppose you have an HTTP servlet that overrides the doGet() method for receiving GET requests. What are the names of the two classes passed into the doGet() method that will allow you to receive requests and to respond to the web client?

Skill Level: Low

Expected answer:

The two object types are HttpServletRequest and HttpServletResponse. The HttpServletRequest object represents the client's request and provides the servlet with access to information about the client, the parameters for the request, and the HTTP headers passed along with the request. The HttpServletResponse object represents the servlet's response and is used to return data to the client.

Here is the signature of an example doGet() method:

```
public void doGet(
   HttpServletRequest req
, HttpServletResponse res
)
throws ServletException, IOException {}
```

Score: _____

Notes: _____

_____

9. Given an HTTP PUT method, what is the corresponding method in the HttpServlet class that will be called upon invocation?

Skill Level: Low

Expected answer:

The doPut() method. The doPut() method of the HttpServlet abstract class is used to handle the HTTP PUT type request.

Score: _____

Notes: _____

_____

10. 10. In a Java Server Page (JSP), how would you declare a String object named firstName and assign it the value of "*Alex*"?

Skill Level: Low

Expected answer:

<%! String firstName = new String("Alex"); %>

Score: _____

Notes: _____

_____

Section average score: _____

Skill Level: _____

J2EE Development Concepts

1. A J2EE application is divided into components based on the function they need to support. What are the components defined in the J2EE specification?

   Skill Level: Low

   Expected answer:

   > Application clients and applets are components that run on the client machine.

   Score: _____

   Notes: _____

   _____

2. Java Servlets and JavaServer Pages (JSP) are web-based components that run within a web container on the server.

   Skill Level: Low

   Expected answer:

   > Enterprise JavaBeans (EJB) components (also known as enterprise beans) are business components that are run within an EJB container on the server.

   Score: _____

   Notes: _____

   _____

3. What is the Remote Method Invocation (RMI) Protocol?

   Skill Level: Intermediate

   Expected answer:

Remote Method Invocation (RMI) is a set of APIs that allows developers to build distributed applications using the Java programming language. Defined in the Java language, RMI uses interfaces to define remote objects with a combination of Java serialization and the Java Remote Method Protocol (JRMP) to turn local method invocations into remote method invocation.

Score: _____

Notes: _____

_____

_____

4. What is the Java Remote Method Protocol (JRMP)?

Skill Level: High

Expected answer:

Java Remote Method Protocol (JRMP) is a proprietary wire-level protocol designed by Sun Microsystems to support the transparent mechanism required for communication between objects in the Java language that reside in different address spaces. The J2EE supports the JRMP protocol but does not appear to use the term any longer; simply referring to it as the "RMI transport protocol". JRMP basically serves the same function as IIOP, but also supports object passing.

Score: _____

Notes: _____

_____

_____

5. What is a deployment descriptor?

Skill Level: Low

Expected answer:

A deployment descriptor is an XML file that accompanies each module of a J2EE application. It describes the specific configuration requirements that need to be resolved for the module or application to be installed successfully to an application server.

Score: _____

Notes: _____

_____

6. J2EE Enterprise Applications, with all of their modules (web, client, business tier), are packaged into what type of file?

Skill Level: Low

Expected answer:

They are packaged into an Enterprise Archive (EAR) file. An EAR file is nothing more than a standard Java Archive (JAR) file with an .ear extension.

Score: _____

Notes: _____

_____

7. What types of files and modules can be found in an Enterprise Archive (EAR) file?

Skill Level: Low

Expected answer:

An EAR file can comprise WAR, EJB JAR, RAR, and JAR files along with the application descriptor file; application.xml.

---

8. What are Web archive (WAR) files? What is the standard file extension to a WAR file?

Skill Level: Low

Expected answer:

A WAR file is used to package *Web modules* for the purpose of deploying them to an application server. A WAR file has a standard file extension .war. A Web Archive (WAR) file is a Java archive file (created using the jar utility) used to store one or more of the following:

- Descriptive meta-information

- Java Servlets

- JavaServer Pages (JSP)

- Utility libraries and classes

- Static documents, such as HTML files, images, and possibly sound files.

- Client-side programs like applets, beans, and classes.

A Web module can represent a stand-alone Web application, or it can be combined with other modules (for example, EJB modules) to form a full J2EE application.

Score: _____

Notes: _____

_____

9. What are the two transport protocols used by J2EE web-based client applications?

Skill Level: Low

Expected answer*:*

Web clients can use either the HTTP or HTTPS transport protocol.

Score: _____

Notes: _____

_____

10. What is the Enterprise Information System (EIS) Tier within the J2EE environment?

Skill Level*:* Intermediate

Expected answer*:*

The EIS tier includes your backend and legacy systems and normally includes the companies' Enterprise Resource Planning (ERP) system, mainframe transaction processing systems, database systems, and other legacy information systems. A typical J2EE enterprise application will need to communicate request and response processing with these legacy systems within the EIS Tier. Integrating new J2EE application with the EIS tier has assumed great importance because enterprises are striving to leverage their existing systems and resources while adopting and developing new technologies and architectures.

Score: _____

Notes: _____

_____

11. What is the standard architecture used for connecting to the Enterprise Information System (EIS) tier from the J2EE platform?

Skill Level: High

Expected answer:

The J2EE Connector Architecture.

Score: _____

Notes: _____

_____

12. What are some of the types of containers defined in the J2EE architecture and what are they used for? Where are they located (client, application server, database server)?

Skill Level: Low

Expected answer:

Application client container - This type of container is found on the client machine and is responsible for running and managing the execution of all application client components for a single J2EE application. An applet container, for example, is a combination of a web browser and Java plug-in located on the client machine.

EJB container - The EJB container is responsible for running and managing the execution of all enterprise beans for a single J2EE application. The EJB container is run on the application server.

Web container - A web container is responsible for running and managing the execution of all JSP and servlet components for a single J2EE application. The web container and its components are run on the application server.

Score: _____

Notes: _____

_____

13. Why would you use a modeling tool for designing a J2EE application?

    Skill Level: Low

    Expected answer:

    > Modeling tools are used to because of the increasing complexity of today's enterprise application systems and their components. These tools allow you to visualize the processes used for constructing and documenting the design and structure of an application. They also provide a means for showing the many components, their interdependencies, and how they relate to other components and subsystems in a large and complex application.

    Score: _____

    Notes: _____

    _____

14. What is the most popular modeling tool used for designing large and complex J2EE applications?

    Skill Level: Low

    Expected answer:

    > The Unified Modeling Language (UML).

15. What is a transaction?

Skill Level: Intermediate

Expected answer:

A transaction is a bracket of processing or a sequence of information exchange and related work that represents a logical unit of work. It can be thought of as an "all or nothing" contract; all of the processing must be completed or else the transaction management component (sometimes called a transaction monitor) should restore (rollback) the application to the status as it was before the start of the transaction.

16. What is ACID as it relates to transactions?

Skill Level: High

Expected answer:

ACID is an acronym used to describe the four primary attributes ensured to any transaction by a transaction manager (sometimes called a transaction monitor or TP monitor). These attributes are:

Atomicity. In a transaction involving two or more discrete pieces of information, either all of the pieces are committed or none are. This is sometimes referred to as the "all-or-nothing" property. This property defines that the entire sequence of operations are successful or the entire sequence is entirely unsuccessful. Successfully completed transactions are committed, while unsuccessful (partially executed) transactions are rolled back.

Consistency. Transaction must always work on a consistent view of data. Also, when a transaction ends, it must leave the data in a consistent state. This property ensures that a transaction never leaves the database in a half-finished state. While a transaction is executing, it may be possible for certain constraints be violated (as with deferred transactions), but no other transaction will be allowed to see these inconsistencies. When the transaction ends, all such inconsistencies will have been eliminated.

Isolation. For a given transaction that is in process and not yet committed, it must remain isolated from any other transaction. This property keeps transactions separated from each other until they're finished. For a given transaction, it should appear as though it is running all by itself — the effects of other concurrently running transactions on the system are invisible to this transaction. The effects of this transaction are invisible to others until the transaction is committed.

Durability. This property defines that the results of any committed data is permanent. Committed data is saved by the system such that, even in the event of a failure and system restart, the data is available in its correct state.

Score: _____

Notes: _____

_____

_____

17. Are JAR files meant to be platform independent?

Skill Level: Low

Expected answer:

Yes. JAR files are based on the popular ZIP file format and are cross-platform so developers do not have to worry about platform issues.

Score: _____

Notes: _____

_____

18. What is the protocol used for communicating between CORBA object request brokers (ORBs)?

Skill Level: Intermediate

Expected answer:

Internet Inter-ORB Protocol (IIOP)

Score: _____

Notes: _____

_____

19. What is Remote Method Invocation (RMI)?

Skill Level: Low

Expected answer:

RMI is a distributed object model that allows a Java object running in one Java Virtual Machine (JVM) to invoke methods on another Java object running in a different JVM.

Score: _____

Notes: _____

_____

20. You are designing a J2EE application that needs to implement asynchronous messaging? Which J2EE service would you use?

Skill Level: Low

Expected answer:

Java Message Service (JMS).

Score: _____

Notes: _____

_____

21. Which J2EE service API would you use to allow applications and J2EE servers to use transactions?

Skill Level: Low

Expected answer*:*

Java Transaction API (JTA).

Score: _____

Notes: _____

_____

Section average score: _____

Skill Level: _____

Java Database Connectivity (JDBC)

1. What is the Java Database Connectivity API?

   Skill Level: Low

   Expected answer:

   The Java Database Connectivity API (or JDBC for short) provides database access to Java applications in a vendor independent manner. When using the JDBC API, a Java application can perform database access independent of the actual database engine. The same Java application can be written once, compiled once, and run against any database engine with a JDBC driver.

   Score: _____

   Notes: _____

   _____

2. The JDBC API consists of which two packages?

   Skill Level: Intermediate

   Expected answer:

   java.sql and javax.sql (which provides for server-side capabilities)

   Score: _____

   Notes: _____

   _____

3. What are the different ways to establish a connection to a database using JDBC?

   Skill Level: High

Expected answer:

Registering the driver using DriverManager.

```
DriverManager.registerDriver(
  new oracle.jdbc.driver.OracleDriver());

Connection con =
  DriverManager.getConnection(
      "jdbc:oracle:thin:@bartman:1521:O920DB"
    , "scott"
    , "tiger");
```

Setting the "jdbc.drivers" system properties.

```
System.setProperty(
    "jdbc.drivers"
  , "oracle.jdbc.driver.OracleDriver");

Connection con =
  DriverManager.getConnection(
      "jdbc:oracle:thin:@bartman:1521:O920DB"
    , "scott"
    , "tiger");
```

Using the classForName method.

```
Class.forName("oracle.jdbc.driver.OracleDriver").newInsta
nce();

Connection con =
  DriverManager.getConnection(
      "jdbc:oracle:thin:@bartman:1521:O920DB"
    , "scott"
    , "tiger");
```

Score: _____

Notes: _____

_____

4. What does it mean when you get a "No suitable driver" error from your JDBC application? What should you look for when approached with this error?

Skill Level: High

Expected answer:

The error, "No suitable driver" typically occurs during a call to the DriverManager.getConnection method. The usual cause can be failing to load the appropriate JDBC drivers before calling the getConnection method. It may also be that you are specifying an invalid JDBC URL - one that isn't recognized by your JDBC driver.

The first thing to check is the documentation for the JDBC driver you are using.

This problem can also be seen when attempting to use the JDBC-ODBC Bridge and one or more of the shared libraries needed by the Bridge cannot be loaded. If you believe this is the case, check your configuration to be sure that any required shared libraries are accessible to the Bridge.

Score:

Notes:

5. You have a JDBC connection object named con. How would you turn off *auto-committing* for this connection?

Skill Level: Low

Expected answer:

Use the setAutoCommit method of the Connection class passing in the boolean value false.

```
con.setAutoCommit(false);
```

Score: _____

Notes: _____

6. You have a ResultSet object named rset that you want to retrieve data from. How would you retrieve all of the data from within a while loop?

Skill Level: Intermediate

Expected answer:

```
String query = "SELECT * FROM my_table";
ResultSet rset = stmt.executeQuery(query);
while (rset.next()) {
  // Use the rset.getXXX methods to
  // retrieve data
}
```

Score: _____

Notes: _____

7. What are some of the getXXX methods in the ResultSet class used to retrieve values?

Skill Level: Low

Expected answer: .

Assuming a ResultSet object named rset, here are some examples:

```
BigDecimal bd = rset.getBigDecimal(1);
Blob       bl = rset.getBlob(2);
boolean    bn = rset.getBoolean(3);
byte   ·   bt = rset.getByte(4);
Clob       cl = rset.getClob(5);
Date       dt = rset.getDate(6);
double     dl = rset.getDouble(7);
float      ft = rset.getFloat(8);
int         i = rset.getInt(9);
```

```
long        l = rset.getLong(10);
short       s = rset.getShort(11);
String      st = rset.getString(12);
```

Score: _____

Notes: _____

_____

_____

8. How would you select an entire row of data from a ResultSet in one command instead of calling an individual ResultSet.getXXX method for each column?

Skill Level: High

Expected answer:

As of the JDBC API 3.0 (at the time of this writing), this is not possible. Using the ResultSet.getXXX methods is the only way to retrieve data from a ResultSet object – this means you will need to make the method call for each column of the row being returned.

Score: _____

Notes: _____

_____

_____

9. Is it possible to get a count of the number of columns returned from a ResultSet object? If so, how?

Skill Level: High

Expected answer:

It is possible to get a column count, but not directly from the ResultSet object. It is possible, however, to instantiate a ResultSetMetaData object (from the ResultSet) and use the getColumnCount() method. The following code provides an example:

```
ResultSet rset =
    stmt.executeQuery("select * from test");

ResultSetMetaData rsMeta = rset.getMetaData();

System.out.println(
    "Number of columns: " +
    rsMeta.getColumnCount()
);
```

Score: _____

Notes: _____

_____

10. Is there a method that could be used to return the number of rows returned from a ResultSet? If so, what is the name of the method? If not, what is the easiest way to capture the number of rows returned?

Skill Level: High

Expected answer:

No. There is no direct method you could call, but it is easy to find the number of rows. Let's say you have a scrollable result set, rset, you can call the methods rset.last and then rset.getRow to find out how many rows rset has. If the result set is not scrollable, you can either (1) count the rows by iterating through the result set or (2) get the number of rows by submitting a query with a COUNT column in the SELECT clause.

Score: _____

Notes: _____

_____

11. You have an application using JDBC connection pooling. Which interface is used as the resource manager connection factory for pooled connection objects (java.sql.Connection objects)?

Skill Level: Intermediate

Expected answer:

PooledConnectionDataSource

Score: _____

Notes: _____

_____

Section average score: _____

Skill Level: _____

Java Servlets

1. What are the two objects passed to the servlet's service method in a servlet that extends the HttpServlet class?

   Skill Level: Low

   Expected answer:

   > The two objects passed are HttpServletRequest and HttpServletResponse. The service method then passes the same two parameters to the appropriate doPut, doGet, or doPost, method in the servlet that extends the HttpServlet class.

   Score: _____

   Notes: _____

   _____

2. What is the name of the *deployment descriptor* for a web application and which directory do you place this file relative to the context (document) root directory?

   Skill Level: Low

   Expected answer:

   > The name of the web application deployment descriptor is named web.xml and is placed in the /WEB-INF/ directory.

   Score: _____

   Notes: _____

   _____

3. What is the corresponding method in the HttpServlet class for an HTTP POST method call?

Skill Level: Low

Expected answer:

doPost

Score: _____

Notes: _____

_____

4. Where should all servlet class files be placed relative to the context (document) root?

Skill Level: Low

Expected answer:

All classes should be placed in the WEB-INF/classes directory.

Score: _____

Notes: _____

_____

5. For a servlet, what method is used to return an Enumeration of String objects that represent the values of all request parameters, as with HTML form parameters?

Skill Level: Intermediate

Expected answer:

You would use the getParameterNames() method of the request object as shown in the following example:

```
Enumeration params =
    req.getParameterNames();
```

6. Servlet containers support the ability to store startup parameters and make them available to the servlet when it is initiated. How would you retrieve an initialization parameter in a servlet?

   Skill Level: Intermediate

   Expected answer:

   You would use two methods: getServletConfig() and getInitParameter("paramName") to return the value as a string as shown in the following example:

   ```
   String myValue =
      getServletConfig().getInitParameter ("myParamName");
   ```

7. How many times does the service method and init method get called for a servlet?

   Skill Level: Low

   Expected answer:

   The service method will be called for every request to the servlet. The init method, on the other hand, is only called one time, and that is when the servlet is being initialized.

8. What is the purpose of the init method of a servlet and what is the parameter passed to the init method?

Skill Level: Low

Expected answer:

> The init method of a servlet is called by the servlet container to indicate to the servlet that it is being placed into service. You can override this method in your servlet to set certain initialization information for your servlet. The init method is passed in a ServletConfig object.

9. Briefly describe the order in which servlets get loaded defined in the deployment descriptor file?

Skill Level: Intermediate

Expected answer:

> The servlet container will first load those servlets that are declared to (have the element) "**load-on-startup**" in the order they are listed in the deployment descriptor. For those servlets that do not have the **load-on-startup** element defined, there is no guarantee when it will be loaded by the servlet container.

10. What is the name of the method and interface used to redirect an HTTP request to another URL?

Skill Level: Low

Expected answer:

You would use the interface / method as a response to the client to redirect it to a new URL:

```
HttpServletResponse.sendRedirect("newUrl")
```

Here is an example:

```
String newUrl = "../RedirectedPage.html";
response.sendRedirect(newUrl);
```

11. You need to write a servlet that prints the name/value pairs of all HTTP request header parameters. Suppose that you already have a PrintWriter object named out and an HttpServletRequest object named request in your servlet. Write the code to print all HTTP request header parameters?

Skill Level: High

Expected answer:

```
...
Enumeration head = request.getHeaderNames();
while (head.hasMoreElements()) {
  String headerName = (String) head.nextElement();
```

```
    String headerValue = request.getHeader(headerName);
    out.println("NAME = " + headerName);
    out.println("VALUE = " + headerValue);
}
...
```

Score: _____

Notes: _____

_____

12. You have a Web application that contains servlets and several Java JAR libraries that are needed to support the application (i.e. JDBC drivers like ojdbc14.jar). Which directory should the Java JAR libraries be placed relative to the context (document) root?

Skill Level: Low

Expected answer:

All JAR files should go in the /WEB-INF/lib/ directory.

Score: _____

Notes: _____

_____

13. What is the name of the XML element defined in the deployment descriptor file that is used by the container to pass initialization parameters to a servlet?

Skill Level: Intermediate

Expected answer:

<init-param>. Here is an example from a web.xml file:

```
<servlet>
  <servlet-name>PrintInitParameters</servlet-name>
  <servlet-class>PrintInitParameters</servlet-class>
  <init-param>
```

```
    <param-name>jdbcClassDriver</param-name>
    <param-value>oracle.jdbc.driver.OracleDriver
    </param-value>
  </init-param>
</servlet>
```

Score: _____

Notes: _____

_____

14. You have an initialization parameter defined in the deployment descriptor (web.xml) for a servlet. How would you retrieve the value of a parameter named "jdbcClassDriver"?

Skill Level: Intermediate

Expected answer:

You would use the:

ServletConfig.getInitParameter("paramName") method as shown in the following example:

```
String jdbcClassDriver =
    getServletConfig().getInitParameter(
        "jdbcClassDriver");
```

Score: _____

Notes: _____

_____

15. You have a servlet where you need to retrieve several servlet initialization parameters from the deployment descriptor. Which method would be best to retrieve the names and values from so that they are only retrieved once, set in a variable global for the servlet? Keep in mind that this is a method that is already being passed the ServletConfig object?

Skill Level: Intermediate

Expected answer:

You would perform the parameter retrieval within the init method of the servlet.

Score: _____

Notes: _____

_____

16. Which method gets called by the servlet container immediately after the servlet is removed from service?

Skill Level: Low

Expected answer:

The destroy method is called.

Score: _____

Notes: _____

_____

17. A web application is a collection of JSP, servlet, HTML, image, JavaBeans, tag libraries, and other class files and libraries. Which object is created and maintained by the servlet container and contains all *context information* about your web application as a whole?

Skill Level: High

Expected answer:

A ServletContext object.

Score: _____

Notes: _____

_____

18. What are context-initialization parameters and how do they different from servlet-initialization parameters?

Skill Level: Low

Expected answer:

Context-initialization parameters (name/value pairs) are those that are defined for the entire context of the application within the web deployment descriptor file. They are said as having *application* scope. This differs from servlet-initialization parameters (again, name/value pairs) that are scoped at the servlet level. They are defined at the servlet level.

Score: _____

Notes: _____

_____

19. What is the name of the XML element used to store context-initialization parameters and which element do they need to be nested in within the web deployment descriptor file?

Skill Level: Intermediate

Expected answer:

Context-initialization parameters are defined in the web deployment descriptor using the <context-param> XML element. They are nested within the root element of the deployment descriptor; <web-app>.

Score: _____

Notes: _____

_____

20. What are the two types of listeners used in a Web application?

Skill Level: Intermediate

Expected answer:

Context attribute listeners and session attribute listeners.

Score: _____

Notes: _____

_____

21. Which interface, defined in the javax.servlet package, needs to be implemented to receive notifications about changes to the servlet context of the web application they are part of? *(For example when servlets are initialized or destroyed)*

Skill Level: High

Expected answer:

The ServletContextListener interface.

Score: _____

Notes: _____

_____

22. Which two methods would you need to implement within the ServletContextListener interface in order to handle the initializing and destroying of a servlet?

Skill Level: High

Expected answer:

The ServletContextListener interface has two methods that need to be implemented in order to handle the events when the web container creates and destroys a servlet:

```
contextInitialized(ServletContextEvent e);
contextDestroyed(ServletContextEvent e):
```

Score: _____

Notes: _____

_____

23. You want to override the attributeAdded method to handle the event of when an attribute is added to a session. Which interface would you find this method in?

Skill Level: High

Expected answer:

The attributeAdded method is defined in the HttpSessionAttributeListener interface.

Score: _____

Notes: _____

_____

24. You are writing a listener to enable you to listen for the notification from the servlet container that a session is being created. What is the name of the interface to implement and the method you need to override to accomplish this?

Skill Level: High

Expected answer:

The name of the interface is javax.servlet.http.HttpSessionListener and the name of the method to override is named sessionCreated.

Score: _____

Notes: _____

_____

_____

25. What is the XML element name and syntax for defining a servlet context listener?

Skill Level: High

Expected answer:

```
<listener>
  <listener-class>
    fully_qualified_class_name
  </listener-class>
</listener>
```

Score: _____

Notes: _____

_____

_____

26. You are writing a servlet that is not thread safe. You would like to have the servlet container execute your servlet by only one thread at a time. Which interface would you implement to make this happen?

Skill Level: Intermediate

Expected answer:

Have your servlet implement the SingleThreadModel. This will tell the servlet container to not allow multiple threads to access the servlet's methods simultaneously.

27. While writing a servlet, you want to write a message out the log file of the web application. What code would you write to log the string "Error Message" to the log file defined by the servlet container?

Skill Level: Intermediate

Expected answer:

```
ServletContext context = getServletContext();
String errorMessage = "Error Message";
context.log(errorMessage);
```

Score: _____

Notes: _____

_____

28. What is the signature of the method of the ServeltContext interface that allows the developer to log a string method and an exception to the log file?

Skill Level: Intermediate

Expected answer:

```
public void log(
         String message
     , Throwable throwable)
```

NOTE: The following signature has been depreciated in favor of the above one:

```
public void log(
         Exception exception
     , String msg)
```

Score: _____

Notes: _____

_____

_____

29. You are developing a servlet that must retain sessions but the policy within the company prohibits cookies being turned on within the browser. Which two methods are available to allow you to put the session ID in the URL?

Skill Level: Intermediate

Expected answer:

```
encodeURL();
encodeRedirectURL();
```

Score: _____

Notes: _____

_____

_____

30. What is the name of the parameter that stores the session ID of a servlet?

Skill Level: Intermediate

Expected answer:

jsessionid

Score: _____

Notes: _____

_____

_____

Section average score: _____

Skill Level: _____

Java Server Pages (JSP)

1. JSP are not directly handled by the application container. What are JSPs converted to so they can be handled by the web application container?

   Skill Level: Low

   Expected answer:

   JSPs are converted to servlets.

   Score: _____

   Notes: _____

   _____

2. Are you supposed to put JSP files in the same directory where Java servlets are stored?

   Skill Level: Low

   Expected answer:

   No. JSP files along with any other static pages (i.e. HTML files) that are to be called directly should be put in the application root directory for the application.

   Score: _____

   Notes: _____

   _____

3. Briefly describe the lifecycle of a JSP?

   Skill Level: Intermediate

   Expected answer:

- **Translate the page**. All tags are converted to Java source code – a servlet.

- **Compile the page**. The Java source code (servlet) is compiled into a class file.

- **Lode the class**. The servlet class gets loaded on its first request from a user.

- **Create an instance of the class**. The servlet container creates an instance of the class.

- **Make call to jspinit**. The servlet container will initialize the servlet instance by calling its jspinit method.

- **Make a call to _jspService**. The servlet container will then make a call to the _jspService method while passing in a *request* and *response* object.

- **Make a call to jspDestroy**. When the container needs to remove the JSP page from service, it will call the jspDestroy method.

Score: _____

Notes: _____

_____

4. Why is the response to a JSP file always slow for the first client request?

Skill Level: Intermediate

Expected answer:

When the JSP page is first called, it must go through a *translate* and *compile* stage which can be resource intensive. After it is converted to a servlet, the loads are very quick.

5. Within a JSP page, you need to declare and initialize a String object named *database* to the value of "*Oracle*". How would you accomplish this?

Skill Level: Low

Expected answer:

```
<%! String database = new String ("Oracle"); %>
```

Score: _____

Notes: _____

_____

6. What are the two types of comments that can be put into a JSP page?

Skill Level: Low

Expected answer:

```
HTML comment: <!-- comment -->
JSP comment: <%-- comment --%>
```

Score: _____

Notes: _____

_____

7. Within a JSP page, you have access to several objects that are implicitly declared. One of those objects is the response object. What are some of the things you can do with this object?

Skill Level: High

Expected answer:

You can use the response object to perform the following:

- Add cookies

- Return an error page

- Add a header

- Redirect the browser to another URL

- Set the HTTP status

Score: _____

Notes: _____

_____

8. How do you *import* other Java class files into your JSP page, just as you would do in a normal Java program?

Skill Level: Low

Expected answer:

You would use the import directive as shown in the following example:

```
<%@ page import="java.util.*;java.sql.*" %>
```

Score: _____

Notes: _____

_____

9. If you have a JSP page that must retain the session of each client, what directive would you set to inform the translation step to instantiate an HttpSession object?

Skill Level: Intermediate

Expected answer:

At the page level, you would set the session attribute to *true* as shown in the following example:

```
<%@ page session="true" %>
```

Score: _____

Notes: _____

_____

10. What is the default value for the session attribute in a JSP page?

Skill Level: Low

Expected answer:

True. If you do not session tracking, you would have to set the session attribute to false:

```
<%@ page session="false" %>
```

Score: _____

Notes: _____

_____

11. In a JSP file, how do you include the contents (source code) of another JSP into your code?

Skill Level: Low

Expected answer:

You would use the include directive as shown in the following example:

```
<%@ include file="myOtherJspFile" %>
```

Score: _____

Notes: _____

_____

_____

12. You have a JavaBean named "com.acme.myBean" that you would like to declare and use in a JSP file. The bean should be scoped for the *page* and the object to be named "myBean". What is the syntax to perform this?

Skill Level: Low

Expected answer:

```
<jsp:useBean
    id="myBean"
    scope="page"
    class="com.acme.myBean"
/>
```

Score: _____

Notes: _____

_____

_____

13. You are using a JavaBean within a JSP and want this same bean object to be shared by different users. What would you set the scope attribute to when declaring the bean in order to allow this?

Skill Level: Intermediate

Expected answer:

You would need to specify the scope attribute as "application" as shown in the following example:

```
<jsp:useBean
    id="myBean"
    scope="application"
    class="com.acme.myBean"
/>
```

Score: _____

Notes: _____

_____

14. You have a JavaBean declared in your JSP page that is named with the ID = "myBean". How would you retrieve the attribute named "amount" from this object given a correctly defined JavaBean?

Skill Level: Low

Expected answer:

Use the following syntax:

```
<jsp:getProperty
    name="myBean"
    property="amount"
/>
```

Score: _____

Notes: _____

_____

15. Which file contains the instructions to the container on where to find tab libraries by mapping a custom tag library URI to the actual tag library file?

Skill Level: Intermediate

Expected answer:

The web deployment descriptor file: web.xml.

16. You want to include a custom tag library in a JSP page. The URI for the library is "/myDBTagLibrary" and the tag prefix you want to use in your JSP page is "db". How would you write the tag library directive in your JSP page to perform this?

Skill Level: Intermedaite

Expected answer:

```
<%@ taglib
    uri="/myDBTagLibrary"
    prefix="db"
%>
```

17. When writing a tag handler Java class, which class do you need to extend?

Skill Level: High

Expected answer:

javax.servlet.jsp.tagext.TagSupport

18. You have just coded and compiled a tag handler Java class to service custom tags in your JSP. Where do you put the tag handler classes?

Skill Level: Intermediate

Expected answer:

The tag handler Java classes should be places in the WEB-INF/classes directory of your web application.

Score: _____

Notes: _____

_____

19. You have a JSP page that is not thread safe. What directive would you set to indicate this in your JSP page?

Skill Level: Intermediate

Expected answer:

You would set the isThreadSafe attribute to false as shown in the following example:

```
<%@ page isThreadSafe="false" %>
```

Score: _____

Notes: _____

_____

20. How do you declare in a JSP page that it should use an error page named "appError.jsp"?

Skill Level: Intermediate

Expected answer:

You would use the following:

```
<%@ page errorPage="appError.jsp" %>
```

Score: _____

Notes: _____

_____

Section average score: _____

Skill Level: _____

Java Beans

1. What is a JavaBean?

   Skill Level: Low

   Expected answer:

   > A JavaBean is specification developed by Sun Microsystems that defines how Java objects interact. Specifically, they are reusable software components written in the Java programming language, designed to be manipulated visually by a software development environment (IDE), like JBuilder, Visual Age for Java, or JDeveloper – basically any application that understands the JavaBeans format.. JavaBeans are very similar to Microsoft's ActiveX components, but designed to be platform-neutral; running anywhere there is a Java Virtual Machine (JVM). JavaBeans can be dropped into an application container, (i.e. a form), and can then be used to perform functions ranging from a simple animation to complex calculations.

   Score: _____

   Notes: _____

   _____

2. How do JavaBeans differ from Enterprise JavaBeans?

   Skill Level: Intermediate

   Expected answer:

   > The JavaBeans architecture is meant to provide a format for general-purpose components within a Java application. They are basically used to *"customize existing objects"*. Think about a button on a form that, when pressed, does not remain pressed – it bounces back to its off state, like a

door-bell. The button acts as a single-state switch. Now you have to create a button that should have two stable states – like a typical light switch. In this case, you can take the existing button (the one having only one stable state) and "customize" it so that it has two stable states.

The Enterprise Java Beans (EJB) architecture, on the other hand, provides a format for highly specialized business (distributed) logic components. It is a completely distinctive concept than the one just mentioned above. EJB's are not used to customize an existing object. Instead they are used to "standardize" the way, in which business logic is written. For example, it is possible to write our business logic within the GUI logic, and also inside Servlets, Applets, and Standalone applications. Unfortunately, there is no clear distinction between the code that is responsible for the GUI and the actual business logic code, because all of the code is written inside the same class files. There is no chance for code reuse. By using EJBs, we can "componentize" the application by writing the business logic into separate class files than the GUI logic. This makes a clear distinction between the responsibilities of the GUI logic and the business logic.

Score: _____

Notes: _____

_____

3. What type of constructor is required for a class to be considered a JavaBean?

Skill Level: Low

Expected answer:

It must have a "no-arg" constructor.

Score: _____

Notes: _____

_____

4. What are the four requirements of a Java class to be considered a JavaBean?

Skill Level: Intermediate

Expected answer:

- The class must contain a no-arg constructor.
- The class will use standardized method names (getter/setter method naming paradigm) for property assessors and mutators.
- There are no public instance variables.
- The class must be public.

Score: _____

Notes: _____

_____

5. You want to include a JavaBean in a JSP page. Which three attributes should be supplied?

Skill Level: Intermediate

Expected answer:

- An ID – which provides a local name for the bean

- The Bean's Class Name – which is used to instantiate the bean if it does not exit

- A Scope – which specifies the lifetime of the bean, which by default is "page"

Score: _____

Notes: _____

_____

6. What would the syntax be if you wanted to include a JavaBean in a JSP with the following attributes:

ID   = "myBean"
Class = "com.acme.MyBean"
Scope = "session"

Skill Level: Low

Expected answer:

```
<jsp:useBean
    id="myBean"
    class="com.mycompany.MyBean"
    scope="session"
/>
```

Score: _____

Notes: _____

_____

7. What are the possible values for the "scope" attribute when initiating a JavaBean within a JSP document using the jsp:useBean action? What is the default value?

Skill Level: Intermediate

Expected answer:

The scope attribute defines the scope within which the reference is available. The possible values are **page**, **request, session**, and **application**. The default for the scope attribute is **page**.

Score: _____

Notes: _____

_____

8. You are using a JavaBean in a JSP and want to provide initial values when the bean gets created. How do you perform this?

Skill Level: High

Expected answer:

You would put the initialization code in the body of the jsp:useBean action tag. The body will not be executed if the bean already exists. Let's look at an example that utilizes the values used in the previous question:

```
<jsp:useBean id="myBean"
             class="com.mycompany.MyBean"
             scope="session">

   <%-- this body is executed only if the
        bean is created. Now let's
        initialize some of the bean
        properties. --%>
   <jsp:setProperty name="myBean"
                    property="prop1"
                    value="123" />
</jsp:useBean>
```

Score: _____

Notes: _____

_____

9. You have included and initiated a JavaBean in a JSP named "myBean". What is the syntax of the action to perform in order to print the value of the property "prop1" to the generated output?

Skill Level: Low

Expected answer:

```
<jsp:getProperty  name="myBean"
                  property="prop1">
```

Score: _____

Notes: _____

_____

_____

10. When you include a JavaBean in a JSP using the jsp:useBean action, it declares a local Java variable to hold the bean object. What is the local Java variable name that it creates?

Skill Level: Intermediate

Expected answer:

The name of the local Java variable that gets created from the jsp:useBean action is exactly the value of the ID attribute. In the action below, a local Java variable named "useBean" will be created.

```
<jsp:useBean
     id="myBean"
     class="com.mycompany.MyBean"
     scope="session"
/>
```

Score: _____

Notes: _____

_____

_____

Section average score: _____

Skill Level: _____

Design Patterns

1. What are Design Patterns?

   Skill Level: Low

   Expected answer:

   Design Patterns are expert solutions or descriptions to recurring software design problems in a given context. They are used to bring together the documentation and core solutions to communicate a given problem and its solution in software design. Design patterns are identified and documented in a form that is easy to distribute, discuss, and understand.

   Score: _____

   Notes: _____

   _____

2. What are some of the benefits of using Design Patterns in Java / J2EE?

   Skill Level: Intermediate

   Expected answer:

   - It is at the core of writing elegant and maintainable code.

   - Improve your system design.

   - Provides for a common vocabulary in discussing and design issues.

   - Provides for the ability to leverage proven and well tested solutions. Most of the common patterns have had many experts around the world testing and proving the solution to the problem.

- Promote design reuse and prevent reinventing the wheel.

- Provide solutions that can be applied to real-world problems.

- Promote class separation. Attempt to keep classes separated and prevent them from having to know too much information about one another.

- Allows you to work better with technologies like J2EE (designing EJBs, Servlets, JSPs, and JMS).

- Patterns can often be used together to solve a much larger problem.

- Can unveil bad practices in existing code or patterns that do not work. An in-depth understanding of design patterns allows the developer to easily refractor code and other design patterns to better solutions.

Score: _____

Notes: _____

_____

3. Most design patterns can be broken into three different types (or categories) of patterns. What are they and briefly describe each of them and their intended benefits?

Skill Level: Intermediate

Expected answer:

- **Creational** – These patterns are concerned with creating object instances for you, rather than having you instantiate objects directly. They allow your programs to be more flexible in deciding which objects need to be created for a given case and not require hard-coding.

- **Structural** – These patterns are concerned with the composition of objects. They allow developers to compose groups of objects into larger structures, such as complex user interfaces or accounting data.

- **Behavioral** – These patterns are concerned with the interaction and responsibility of objects. They assist the developer in defining communication between objects in a system and how the flow is controlled in a complex program.

Score: _____

Notes: _____

_____

4. What design pattern does the Struts framework adhere to?

Skill Level: Low

Expected answer:

The Struts application framework adheres to the MVC design pattern. This framework is used when development web components consisting of JSPs and servlets.

Score: _____

Notes: _____

_____

5. Briefly describe the Abstract Factory Method including its intent?

Skill Level: Intermediate

Expected answer:

The Abstract Factory Method provides in interface used to create and return families of related or dependent objects without actually specifying their concrete class. This pattern is used when you want to return one of several related classes of objects, each of which can return several different objects on request. It is often helpful to think of the Abstract Factory as a pattern as a factory object that returns one of several other factories.

Score: _____

Notes: _____

_____

6. What is a Session Facade?

Skill Level: High

Expected answer:

A Session Facade is a pattern commonly used when developing enterprise applications with the intent of defining a higher-level business component that contains and centralizes complex interactions between lower-level business components (i.e. Entity beans and other session beans). A Session Facade is implemented as a session enterprise bean and provides clients with a single interface for the functionality of an application or application subset. They also allow the developer to decouple lower-level business components from one another, making the system design more flexible and comprehensible.

Think about a banking application that has the option of allowing a customer to transfer a balance from one account to another. Visualize the application (client) as needing to check if the user is authorized, get the status of both accounts, check that there is enough money in the first account, and then finally perform the transfer of funds. This all needs to take place in a single transaction – if something goes wrong, the transaction need to be rolled back. As you can see, there can be multiple server side components (EJBs) that need to be accessed / modified. All of these invocations from the client can cause a tremendous amount of network traffic, poor reusability, high coupling, code maintainability, and performance problems because of the high latency of the remote calls from the client. Using a Session Facade design pattern, you can wrap all of the calls (invocations) into a single Session Bean, so the client will have a single point to access (that is the session bean) that will take care of handling all the rest.

Score: _____

Notes: _____

_____

7. What is a Singleton and why would you use this design pattern?

Skill Level: Intermediate

Expected answer:

The Singleton design pattern one of the "creational patterns" and is intended to ensure that a class has only one instance and also provides for a global point to access it from. Many applications that have only one window manager or print spooler or a single point of access to a relational database may need to prevent from having multiple instances.

Score: _____

Notes: _____

_____

8. What is the Iterator Design Pattern?

Skill Level: Low

Expected answer:

Probably one of the easiest and most widely used, the Iterator design pattern allows you to move through (access) a group of elements of an aggregate object (i.e. a list of collection) using a standard interface without having to know the details of its underlying implementation or the internal representations of the data. The developer can also create special iterators that perform some special processing (filtering) to only return specified elements of a data collection.

Score: _____

Notes: _____

_____

9. What are the two J2SE APIs associated with the Iterator design pattern?

Skill Level: Low

Expected answer:

```
java.util.Iterator
java.util.Enumeration
```

10. Which two packages in J2SE includes the Decorator pattern?

    Skill Level: High

    Expected answer:

    The Decorator pattern is actually found in two different packages: java.io and java.awt.

11. What design pattern would you use as an alternative to sub-classing when you need to extend the functionality of an object dynamically?

    Skill Level: High

    Expected answer:

    You could use the Decorator design pattern. The Decorator uses composition rather than inheritance to extend the functionality of an object during runtime.

12. You have a situation where you need to make a change to an object that requires making changes to other objects, and the

number of objects that need to be changed are not known. The object needs to *notify* all other required objects but cannot make any assumptions about the identity of those objects. Which design pattern would you use?

Skill Level: High

Expected answer*:*

In this situation, it would be best to use the Observer design pattern. This design pattern defines a "one-to-many" dependency that provides for the ability to have all of its children objects notified and changed automatically when the parent is changed.

Score: _____

Notes: _____

_____

13. You have an application that uses a significant amount of objects. What design patter would you use if the resource cost are high because of the number of objects and you do not care about the identity of the object?

Skill Level: High

Expected answer*:*

The proper design pattern to use would be the Flyweight design pattern.

Score: _____

Notes: _____

_____

14. Consider an application that has to create a complex object and requires an algorithm that can create this object without

being dependent on the components that comprise the object and how they are assembled. Which design patter would be most appropriate for this?

Skill Level: High

Expected answer:

The Builder Design Pattern.

Score: _____

Notes: _____

_____

15. What are the methods defined in the Iterator class?

Skill Level: Intermediate

Expected answer:

```
hasNext()
next()
remove()
```

Score: _____

Notes: _____

_____

Section average score: _____

Skill Level: _____

Enterprise Java Beans (EJB)

1. What is an Enterprise Java Bean?

   Skill Level: Low

   Expected answer*:*

   > An Enterprise Java Bean (EJB) is component based architecture within the J2EE APIs that is used for developing and deploying component-based distributed business (enterprise) applications. It should contain the business logic for an application and is the heart of most J2EE applications.

   Score: _____

   Notes: _____

   _____

2. What are the three types of EJBs defined in the J2EE specification?

   Skill Level: Low

   Expected answer:

   - Session Bean
   - Entity Bean
   - Message-Driven Bean

   Score: _____

   Notes: _____

   _____

3. You are tasked with writing an EJB that needs to act as a listener for the Java Messaging Service API and processes

message asynchronously. Which type of EJB would you create?

Skill Level: Low

Expected answer:

A message-driven bean.

Score: _____

Notes: _____

_____

4. For an EJB, which software component provides for its transaction management, resource pooling, transaction management, and security checks?

Skill Level: Low

Expected answer:

An EJB container, which is one of the components of a J2EE application server.

Score: _____

Notes: _____

_____

5. What are some of the J2EE APIs an EJB container must support?

Skill Level: Low

Expected answer:

J2SE, JNDI, JMS, JavaMail, JAF, RMI-IIOP, JTA, JAAS, and JDBC.

Score: _____

Notes: _____

_____

6. What are the three class/interfaces that every EJB must have coded, as defined in the J2EE specification?

Skill Level: Intermediate

Expected answer:

- Home Interface
- Remote Interface
- The Bean Class (Session or Entity Bean)

Score: _____

Notes: _____

_____

7. You are developing a Session Bean and have already coded the *Home* and *Remote* interface and are now developing the Java Bean class. Which interface do you have to implement in the session bean class?

Skill Level: Intermediate

Expected answer:

`javax.ejb.SesionBean`

Score: _____

Notes: _____

_____

8. Which kind of methods go into the remote interface for an EJB?

Skill Level: Intermediate

Expected answer:

The remote interface is developed by the bean developer and should contain the business methods that can be called by the client. The remote interface actually acts as a proxy.

Score: _____

Notes: _____

_____

9. When developing the remote interface, which interface much it extend?

Skill Level: Low

Expected answer:

The remote interface should extend the javax.ejb.EJBObject interface.

Score: _____

Notes: _____

_____

10. When developing the Home interface, which interface much it extend?

Skill Level: Low

Expected answer:

The home interface should extend the javax.ejb.EJBHome interface.

11. What is the purpose of the Home interface in an EJB?

Skill Level: Low

Expected answer:

The home interface acts as a factory pattern and defines the methods that allow the client to create instances of the EJB as well as finding or removing an entity bean.

12. What are the two types of Session Beans?

Skill Level: Low

Expected answer:

- Stateless Session Beans
- Stateful Session Beans

13. What is the difference between a stateful session bean and a stateless session bean?

Skill Level: Intermediate

Expected answer:

A *stateless bean* does not hold any conversational state for a calling client's session. It is important to understand that technically, a stateless bean "may" hold state, but it is not guaranteed to be specific to the calling client. A stateless bean is appropriate for application business logic that does not need to hold the value of its instance variables for a client.

A *stateful bean*, on the other hand, is designed to retain its state for the duration of the client-bean session. The state of an object retained by the values of its instance variables. The instance variables are what represent the state of a unique client-bean session. When the client terminates (or removes) the bean, the session ends and its state no longer exists.

Score: _____

Notes: _____

_____

14. You need to write an EJB that must permanently persist data to a secondary storage device. Which type of bean would be most appropriate for this type of application?

Skill Level: Low

Expected answer:

An entity bean.

Score: _____

Notes: _____

_____

15. What is the purpose of Passivation of an EJB?

Expected answer:

Passivation is a resource management technique to help in reducing the number if bean instances running on the system in order to conserve memory. The container will write the state of a bean to the file system in order for the instance of the bean to be used by another session.

Score: _____

Notes: _____

_____

16. Passivation is only available with which two types of beans?

Skill Level: Intermediate

Expected answer:

Entity beans and stateful session beans.

Score: _____

Notes: _____

_____

17. Is it a requirement that an entity bean have a unique object identifier? If yes, then what is this unique identifier commonly called?

Skill Level: Low

Expected answer:

Yes. Each entity bean must have a unique object identifier. This unique identifier is commonly called the bean's *primary key*.

Score: _____

Notes: _____

_____

18. What is the difference between container-managed and bean-managed persistence? Which type of EJB does this refer to?

Skill Level: Low

Expected answer:

Let's first answer the second question – the idea of managed persistence refers to *entity beans*.

With *container-managed persistence*, the EJB container is responsible for saving the state of the bean. The bean's code will contain no database access code (SQL) to manage its state. The fields required for container-managed storage need to be specified in the deployment descriptor and the persistence is handled automatically by the container.

Bean-managed persistence, on the other hand, requires the developer of the entity bean to write the database access calls (SQL) code to retain its own state. The container will not generate any database code to assist in saving the state of the entity bean. This type of implementation is obviously less adaptable than container-managed persistence and needs to be hand-coded into the bean by the developer.

Score: _____

Notes: _____

_____

19. Why would you use bean pooling?

Expected answer:

EJBs are heavyweight components that require considerable system resources to create and destroy. It is advantageous for the container to manage a pool of EJBs that users will be able to use throughout the entire application. By having a bean pool in place, the container will be able to handle more user requests since it will not be wasting time and resources creating and destroying objects. The pool of beans will be shared in an efficient way by all users of the system.

Score: _____

Notes: _____

_____

20. You have to write a bean that is involved with mostly workflow of a system and you need to use the lightest weight EJB, which type of bean would you choose?

Skill Level: Intermediate

Expected answer:

A stateless session bean.

Score: _____

Notes: _____

_____

21. Can a single message-driven bean instance process messages from multiple clients?

Skill Level: Intermediate

Expected answer:

Yes. All instances of a bean are equivalent. This allows the bean container to assign a message to any message-driven bean instance.

Score: _____

Notes: _____

_____

22. Does a message-driven bean's instance retain any data or conversational state for a specific client?

Skill Level: Intermediate

Expected answer:

No.

Score: _____

Notes: _____

_____

23. What are the only types of messages that can be processed by a message-driven bean as of the 1.3 release of the J2EE specification?

Skill Level: Low

Expected answer:

Message-driven beans can only process JMS messages. This may change in future release to process other kinds of messages.

Score: _____

Notes: _____

_____

24. What is the name and type of file used for an EJB deployment descriptor?

Skill Level: Low

Expected answer:

An XML file named ejb-jar.xml.

Score: _____

Notes: _____

_____

25. What is the root element in an EJB deployment descriptor?

Skill Level: Intermediate

Expected answer:

<ejb-jar>. All other elements must be nest within the <ejb-jar> tag.

Score: _____

Notes: _____

_____

26. Consider a Container-managed bean that has data that needs to be compressed or reformatted before saving to the database. Which method will the container call to perform this action before saving?

Skill Level: High

Expected answer:

The ejbStore method is called by the container before saving to the database for the purpose of compressing or reformatting.

Score: _____

Notes: _____

_____

_____

27. You have a transactional client attempting to invoke an EJB method whose transactional attribute is set to 'NEVER' within a transaction context. What will happen?

Skill Level: High

Expected answer:

A RemoteException is thrown to the calling client. Setting the transactional attribute of an EJB method to 'NEVER' means that the bean method should never be invoked within the scope of a transaction.

Score: _____

Notes: _____

_____

_____

28. Within the lifecycle of a stateless session bean, how many times does the ejbRemove method get invoked?

Skill Level: Low

Expected answer:

Only once.

Score: _____

Notes: _____

_____

29. To access an entity bean, which class is used to lookup the home object of an enterprise bean?

Skill Level: Intermediate

Expected answer:

The InitialContext class. When accessing an entity bean, the client needs to start a JNDI connection to obtain a directory connection to the bean's container. Once this connection is established, you will then create an InitialContext object. This object is then used to lookup the bean.

Score: _____

Notes: _____

_____

Section average score: _____

Skill Level: _____

Java Message Service (JMS)

1. What is the Java Messaging Service (JMS)?

   Skill Level: Low

   Expected answer:

   > The Java Messaging Service (JMS) is a J2EE service that enables support to exchange messages between Java programs. This allows applications can create, send, receive, and read messages. JMS provides support for asynchronous communication in Java. The sender and receiver do not have to know anything about each other – both the sender and receiver can operate independently.

   Score: _____

   Notes: _____

   _____

2. Which package would you find the JMS APIs?

   Skill Level: Low

   Expected answer:

   > javax.jms

   Score: _____

   Notes: _____

   _____

3. Why would you choose messaging over other Java technologies like Remote Method Invocation (RMI) in an application?

   Skill Level: Intermediate

Expected answer:

Java Messaging Service (JMS) is a very "loosely coupled" technology while RMI is a very "tightly coupled" technology.

You may have an application where the provider does not want the components to depend on information about other components' interfaces, so that application components can be easily swapped out.

Also, the provider may want the application to run whether or not all components are up and running simultaneously.

Lastly, the application model may want to allow a component to send information (messages) to another component and to continue execution without receiving an immediate response.

Score: _____

Notes: _____

_____

4. Which type of Enterprise Java Bean (EJB) was introduced to allow J2EE applications to process messages asynchronously?

Skill Level: Low

Expected answer:

Message-Driven Bean.

Score: _____

Notes: _____

_____

5. What are the two different types of message domains (sometimes called messaging models) that are supported by the JMS specification?

Skill Level: Low

Expected answer:

[1] Point-to-point – (Queue) and [2] Publish-and-Subscribe – (Topic).

Score: _____

Notes: _____

_____

6. Briefly describe the two types of message domains (sometimes called messaging models) defined in the JMS specification. Try to explain any timing dependency differences between the two.

Skill Level: Low

Expected answer:

Point-to-point – (Queue):

Point-to-point is built around the concept of message queues, senders, and receivers. A *message producer* sends a message to a specific queue. A *message consumer* can attach itself (connect) to a queue and listen for messages. When a message arrives on the queue, the consumer removes it from the queue and responds to it. Each message can have only one consumer. There are no timing dependencies for a producer and receiver of a message. It is possible for a receiver to receive a message whether or not it was running when the producer sent the message. A message can be sent to just one queue and will be processed by just one consumer. When the consumer reads the message, it will acknowledge the successful processing of the message.

Publish-and-Subscribe – (Topic):

In a Publish-and-Subscribe message domain, producers send messages to a *topic*. All of the registered consumers for that topic can retrieve those messages. Using Publish-and-Subscribe, many consumers can receive the same message. The system will take care of distributing messages arriving from a topic's multiple publishers to its multiple subscribers. Keep in mind that publishers and subscribers have timing dependencies. An application that subscribes to a topic can only consume messages published "after" the client has created a subscription and the subscriber is active before that time.

Score: _____

Notes: _____

_____

7. With the Point-to-Point message domain, can a consumer filter messages it receives? How? Where does the filtering get performed?

Skill Level: High

Expected answer:

Yes. Consumers can filter messages by using a *Message Selector*. This is done using a SQL-92 grammar which allows a message consumer to specify the messages it is interested in. Message selectors will assign the work of filtering messages to the JMS provider rather than to the application.

A message selector is a String object that contains an expression based on a subset of the SQL-92 conditional expression syntax. The methods createReceiver, createSubscriber, and createDurableSubscriber each have a form that allows the developer to specify a message selector as an argument when you create a message consumer. The message consumer will then only receive messages whose headers and properties match the selector. Here are several examples:

```
phone LIKE '412'
price BETWEEN 50 AND 100
name IN('Jeff','Alex')
JMSType IS NOT NULL
```

Score: _____

Notes: _____

_____

8. When using a Message Selector, can it filter messages based on the contents of the message body?

Skill Level: Intermediate

Expected answer:

No. A message selector cannot select messages on the basis of the content of the message body – only based on the header and properties of the message.

Score: _____

Notes: _____

_____

9. The Publish-and-Subscriber messaging domain defines a timing constraint between publishers and subscribers, where the subscriber has to be active at the time a message is

produced in order to receive it. How does the JMS API relax this timing dependency?

Skill Level: High

Expected answer:

The client can create a *durable subscription*. A durable subscription can receive messages sent even when the subscribers are not active. This allows for a messaging model that allows clients to send messages to many recipients without the timing constraints imposed by the default nature of publish-and-subscriber.

Score: _____

Notes: _____

_____

10. What are the three components of a Message?

Skill Level: Low

Expected answer:

- Header
- Properties
- Body

Score: _____

Notes: _____

_____

11. What kind of information is found in the header of a Message?

Skill Level: Intermediate

Expected answer:

The header of a message contains message identification and routing information. This includes, but is not limited to:

- JMSDestination
- JMSDeliveryMode
- JMSMessageID
- JMSTimeStamp
- JMSExpiration
- JMSReplyTo
- JMSCorrelationID
- JMSType
- JMSRedelivered

Score: _____

Notes: _____

_____

12. Describe the 5 message body formats (also called message types) defined in the JMS API?

Skill Level: Low

Expected answer:

- **StreamMessage:** A stream of primitive values in the Java that is filled and read sequentially.

- **MapMessage:** Holds a set of name/value pairs where the names are String's and the values are primitive types defined in Java. The entries can be read either sequentially by an enumerator or randomly by name. There is no order defined for this type of message.

- **BytesMessage**: A stream of non-interpreted bytes of type byte[]. Used for encoding a body to math an existing message format.

- **TextMessage**: A java.lang.String object. (i.e. an XML, CSV or HTML file)

- **ObjectMessage**: A serialized object. Of type Object.

Score: _____

Notes: _____

_____

13. You are about to create a QueueSession object (javax.jms.QueueSession). Which object is used to create a QueueSession object?

Skill Level: Intermediate

Expected answer:

A QueueSession object is created from a QueueConnection object as show in the following snippet:

```
queueConnection =
 queueConnectionFactory.createQueueConnection();
queueSession =
    queueConnection.createQueueSession(
        false
      , Session.AUTO_ACKNOWLEDGE
    );
```

Score: _____

Notes: _____

_____

14. What are some of the things a QueueSession is responsible for creating?

Skill Level: Intermediate

Expected answer:

- Messages
- Senders
- Receivers
- Transactions

Score: _____

Notes: _____

_____

15. You have a QueueSession object named queueSession and want to create a *Text Message Type* named textMessage. What would the syntax be?

Skill Level: Intermediate

Expected answer:

```
TextMessage message =
    queueSession.createTextMessage();
```

Score: _____

Notes: _____

_____

16. Is a QueueSession object single or multi-threaded?

Skill Level: Low

Expected answer:

> Single threaded. Any message sending and receiving happens in a well-defined serial order.

> Score: _____

> Notes: _____

> _____

17. You have a TextMessage object named message. How would you assign the content (body) of the message to "Test Message"?

Skill Level: Low

Expected answer:

```
TextMessage message =
    queueSession.createTextMessage();

message.setText("Test Message");
```

> Score: _____

> Notes: _____

> _____

18. Message consumer clients can receive messages in two different way; blocking and non-blocking. What are the two methods of javax.jms.MessageConsumer used to receive messages in blocking and non-blocking mode?

Skill Level: Low

Expected answer:

> Blocking mode: `receive()`
> Non-blocking mode: `receiveNoWait()`

Score: _____

Notes: _____

_____

19. In the javax.jms.MessageConsumer class, what does the method receive(long) do?

Skill Level*:* Intermediate

Expected answer*:*

Notice that the receive method takes one argument – a Java long. This method will retrieve the next message that arrives within the specified timeout interval (defined by the value of the long passed in). This call will block until a message arrives, the timeout expires, or this message consumer is closed.

Score: _____

Notes: _____

_____

20. Given the method javax.jms.MessageConsumer.receive(long), what value would you pass so that the call will block indefinitely and never timeout?

Skill Level: High

Expected answer*:*

Pass in the value zero.

Score: _____

Notes: _____

_____

21. Describe the lifecycle of a JMS Sender application by explaining the steps you would need to perform in order to send a message.

Skill Level: Intermediate

Expected answer:

- Use the JNDI to get a ConnectionFactory and Destination object. (either Queue or Topic)

- Create a Connection object.

- Create a Session object in order for sending/receiver messages.

- Create a MessageProducer object. (either a TopicPublisher or QueueSender)

- Start the connection.

- Send (publish) the message to its destination.

- Close the session and connection.

Score: _____

Notes: _____

_____

22. Describe the lifecycle of a JMS Receiver application by explaining the steps you would need to perform in order to receive a message that will block?

Skill Level: Intermediate

Expected answer:

- Use the JNDI to get a ConnectionFactory and Destination object. (either Queue or Topic)

- Create a Connection object.

- Create a Session object in order for sending/receiver messages.

- Create a MessageConsumer object. (either a TopicSubscriber or QueueReceiver)

- Start the connection.

- Receive the message.

- Close the session and connection.

Score: _____

Notes: _____

_____

23. Messages are not considered successful until they have been acknowledged. What are the four types of acknowledgment?

Skill Level: High

Expected answer:

- **Acknowledgement by commit**. This is the only type allowed in a transacted sessions. In this case, acknowledgment happens automatically when a transaction is committed.

- **Session.AUTO_ACKNOWLEDGE**. Passed as the second argument to the createQueueSession method, the session will automatically acknowledge upon successful return from MessageConsumer.receive() or MessageListener.onMessage() method call.

- **Session.CLIENT_ACKNOWLEDGE**. Passed as the second argument to the createQueueSession method, the client must call the acknowledge() method of Message object.

- **Session.DUPS_OK_ACKNOWLEDGE.** Passed as the second argument to the createQueueSession method, this is sometimes referred to as early acknowledgement. It instructs the session to simply acknowledge the message after it has been delivered. This is likely to result in the delivery of some duplicate messages if the JMS provider fails. Consumers need to be able to tolerate duplicate messages.

Score: _____

Notes: _____

_____

24. As it relates to acknowledgement, what happens to messages if a transaction is rolled back?

Skill Level: Intermediate

Expected answer:

If a transaction is rolled back, all consumed messages are re-delivered.

Score: _____

Notes: _____

_____

25. Which J2EE service is used to manage distributed transactions in a JMS application?

Skill Level: Low

Expected answer:

Java Transaction API (JTA)

Score: _____

Notes: _____

_____

_____

Section average score: _____

Skill Level: _____

Oracle PL/SQL Job Interview Questions

1. Describe the difference between a procedure, function, and anonymous PL/SQL block.

   Skill Level: Low

   Expected answer:

   > Candidate should mention use of the DECLARE statement. A function must return a value while a procedure doesn't have to.

   Score: _____

   Notes: _____

   _____

2. What is a mutating table error and how can you get around it?

   Skill Level: Intermediate

   Expected answer:

   > This happens with triggers. It occurs because the trigger is trying to modify a row it is currently using. The usual fix involves either use of views or temporary tables so the database is selecting from one while updating the other.

   Score: _____

   Notes: _____

   _____

3. Describe the use of %ROWTYPE and %TYPE in PL/SQL.

   Skill Level: Low

Expected answer:

%ROWTYPE allows you to associate a variable with an entire table row. The %TYPE associates a variable with a single column type.

Score: _____

Notes: _____

_____

4. What packages (if any) has Oracle provided for use by developers?

Skill Level: Intermediate to High

Expected answer:

Oracle provides the DBMS_ series of packages. There are many which developers should be aware of, such as *dbms_sql, dbms_pipe, dbms_transaction, dbms_lock, dbms_alert, dbms_output, dbms_job, dbms_utility, dbms_ddl, utl_file*. If they can mention a few of these and describe how they used them, even better. If they include the SQL routines provided by Oracle, great, but that is not really what was asked.

Score: _____

Notes: _____

_____

5. Describe the use of PL/SQL tables.

Skill Level: Intermediate

Expected answer:

PL/SQL tables are scalar arrays that can be referenced by a binary integer. They can be used to hold values for use in later queries or calculations. In Oracle 8, they will be able to be of the %ROWTYPE designation, or RECORD.

Score: _____

Notes: _____

_____

6. When is a declare statement needed?

Skill Level: Low

Expected answer:

The DECLARE statement is used in PL/SQL anonymous blocks, such as stand-alone, non-stored PL/SQL procedures. It must come first in a PL/SQL stand-alone file, if it is used.

Score: _____

Notes: _____

_____

7. In what order should an open/fetch/loop set of commands in a PL/SQL block be implemented if you use the %NOTFOUND cursor variable in the exit when statement? Why?

Skill Level: Intermediate

Expected answer:

OPEN then FETCH then LOOP followed by the exit when. If not specified in this order, it will result in the final return being done twice because of the way the %NOTFOUND is handled by PL/SQL.

Score: _____

Notes: _____

         _____

8. What are SQLCODE and SQLERRM and why are they important for PL/SQL developers?

Skill Level: Intermediate

Expected answer:

SQLCODE returns the value of the error number for the last error encountered. The SQLERRM returns the actual error message for the last error encountered. They can be used in exception handling to report, or store in an error log table, the error that occurred in the code. These are especially useful for the WHEN OTHERS exception.

Score: _____

Notes: _____

         _____

9. How can you find out if a cursor is open within a PL/SQL block?

Skill Level: Low

Expected answer: Use the %ISOPEN cursor status variable.

Score: _____

Notes: _____

         _____

10. How can you generate debugging output from PL/SQL?

Skill Level: Intermediate to High

Expected answer:

Use the *dbms_output* package. Another possible method is to just use the SHOW ERROR command, but this only shows errors. The *dbms_output* package can be used to show intermediate results from loops and the status of variables as the procedure is executed. The new package *utl_file* can also be used.

Score: _____

Notes: _____

_____

11. What are the types of table triggers?

Skill Level: Intermediate to High

Expected Answer:

There are 12 types of triggers in PL/SQL that consist of combinations of the BEFORE, AFTER, ROW, TABLE, INSERT, UPDATE, DELETE, and EACH key word. There are also system-level triggers for DDL, server errors, database startup/shutdown, and user login and logoff triggers.

BEFORE ALL ROW INSERT
AFTER ALL ROW INSERT
BEFORE INSERT
AFTER INSERT
Etc.

Score: _____

Notes: _____

_____

Section average score: _____

Skill Level: _____

UNIX Interview Questions

The command line drives the UNIX operating system. An in-depth knowledge of the available commands is fundamental for working with a UNIX OS. In addition, knowledge of the file system is crucial since everything in UNIX is a file. The following questions can be used to easily differentiate an experienced UNIX sysadmin from a trainee.

1. What are the fields defined in the /etc/passwd file?

   Skill level: Intermediate

   Expected answer:

   - Field 1: username
   - Field 2: placeholder for encrypted password (assuming shadow passwords are being used)
   - Field 3: UID (User Identification)
   - Field 4: GID (Group Identification)
   - Field 5: Comment
   - Field 6: Home directory
   - Field 7: Login shell

   Score: _____

   Notes: _____

   _____

2. What is the purpose of the 'grep' command?

   Skill level: Low

   Expected answer:

   grep is used to search for strings of text in files. Grep stands for 'Global Regular Expression Print'

Score: _____

Notes: _____

_____

3. What command is used to display information about the network interfaces on a system?

Skill level: Low

Expected answer:

ifconfig

Score: _____

Notes: _____

_____

4. The 'ps' command lists processes currently running on the system. Identify and describe the following column headers from the output of 'ps -aef':

- UID

- PID

- PPID

- TTY

Skill level: Intermediate

Expected answer:

- UID = User Identification, the owner of the process

- PID = Process ID. Each UNIX process is assigned a unique process ID.

- PPID = Parent Process ID. The PID of the parent of this process.

Conducting the Programmer Job Interview

- TTY = On what terminal is this process running. If the TTY is "?", then the process is not running on a terminal (either a system process or a detached process).

Score: _____

Notes: _____

_____

5. In Solaris, what command is used to display the slice information for a particular disk?

Skill level: Low

Expected answer:

prtvtoc <device>

Score: _____

Notes: _____

_____

6. What command is used to display the disk space occupied by mounted file systems?

Skill level: Low

Expected answer:

df

Score: _____

Notes: _____

_____

7. What file contains a list of currently mounted file systems?

Skill level: Intermediate

Expected answer:

> /etc/mtab (on Linux)
> /etc/mnttab (on Solaris)

Score: _____

Notes: _____

_____

8. On Solaris, what file contains settings that define the default maximum time a password is valid and the default minimum time period before a password must be changed?

Skill level: Intermediate

Expected answer:

> /etc/default/passwd

Score: _____

Notes: _____

_____

9. What command and options would you issue to set the permissions on a file to read, write, excute for owner, read and execute for group, and no permissions for other?

Skill level: Intermediate

Expected answer:

> chmod 750 <filename>

10. What command will display the default file permissions that will be assigned when a user creates a file?

Skill level: Intermediate

Expected answer:

    umask

Score: _____

Notes: _____

    _____

11. On Solaris, what command is used to display the Access Control List entries for a file?

Skill level: Intermediate

Expected answer:

    getfacl <filename>

Score: _____

Notes: _____

    _____

12. What command is used to run an application with a different security context than the user's default? What is the configuration file for this command, where programs are listed which defined users can execute with higher privileges?

Skill level: Intermediate

Expected answer:

    sudo <program>
    /etc/sudoers

Score: _____

Notes: _____

_____

13. What file defines the default run level of the system and dictates what directory holds the startup scripts for that run level?

    Skill level: Low

    Expected answer:

    /etc/inittab

    Score: _____

    Notes: _____

    _____

14. What command is used to check a file system for errors?

    Skill level: Low

    Expected answer:

    fsck

    Score: _____

    Notes: _____

    _____

15. Why are there normally two bin directories, /bin and /usr/bin?

    Skill level: Intermediate

Expected answer:

The UNIX file system was designed to be shared by multiple systems. In a shared environment, it is unnecessary to have data duplication across multiple systems. The /usr partition on a UNIX system is designed to be shared by clients. This is normally accomplished by client systems mounting a server's /usr partition as their own. This way, all clients have access to the same programs without a system administrator having to maintain copies on multiple systems.

Because of this fact, files in the /usr partition must never be considered critical system files. If a client needs to boot up off of the network for some reason, they will not have access to their /usr partition if it is mounted from a central server. If some sort of system repair ability is necessary on a client system, that program needs to live in the /bin directory. By convention, the /bin directory is local to every system.

So the reason there are two bin directories is that /bin contains local system-level binaries that are critical for the correct operation of the system, while /usr/bin contains binaries that are less important and not critical to the basic functioning of the system.

Score: _____

Notes: _____

_____

16. On Solaris, what file defines the master kernel configuration file?

Skill level: Low

Expected answer:

/etc/system

Score: _____

Notes: _____

_____

17. At the Solaris OpenBoot prompt, what command will display all of the SCSI devices connected to the system?

Skill level: Intermediate

Expected answer:

probe-scsi

Score: _____

Notes: _____

_____

18. How do you boot a Solaris system into single user mode?

Skill level: Low

Expected answer:

- Get to the OpenBoot prompt by hitting Stop-A

- Boot the system with the command 'boot -s'

Score: _____

Notes: _____

_____

19. What command allows you display and to modify your keyboard mappings in X Windows?

Skill level: Intermediate

Expected answer:

xmodmap

Score: _____

Notes: _____

_____

20. In Linux, what file contains a list of all IRQs currently in use?

Skill level: High

Expected answer:

/proc/interrupts

Score: _____

Notes: _____

_____

Section average score: _____

Skill Level: _____

Data Modeling Interview Questions

1. Describe third normal form?

   Skill Level: Low

   Expected answer:

   > Something like: In third normal form, all attributes in an entity are related to the primary key and only to the primary key.

   Score: _____

   Notes: _____

   _____

2. Is the following statement true or false?

   "All relational databases must be in third normal form."

   Why or why not?

   Skill Level: Intermediate

   Expected answer:

   > False. While 3NF is good for logical design, most databases, if they have more than just a few tables, will not perform well using full 3NF. Usually, some entities will be de-normalized in the logical to physical transfer process.

   Score: _____

   Notes: _____

   _____

3. What is an ERD?

   Skill Level: Low

Expected answer:

An ERD is an Entity-Relationship-Diagram. It is used to show the entities and relationships for a database logical model.

Score: _____

Notes: _____

_____

4. Why are recursive relationships bad? How do you resolve them?

Skill Level: Intermediate

Expected answer:

A recursive relationship (one where a table relates to itself) is bad when it is a hard relationship (i.e. neither side is a "may" both are a "must"), as this can result in it not being possible to put in a top or perhaps a bottom of the table. (For example, in the EMPLOYEE table you could not put in the PRESIDENT of the company because he has no boss or the junior janitor because he has no subordinates). These types of relationships are usually resolved by adding a small intersection entity.

Score: _____

Notes: _____

_____

5. What does a hard one-to-one relationship mean (one where the relationship on both ends is "must")?

Skill Level: Low to Intermediate

Expected answer:

> This means the two entities should probably be made into one entity.

Score: _____

Notes: _____

_____

6. How should a many-to-many relationship be handled?

Skill Level: Intermediate

Expected answer: By adding an intersection entity table

Score: _____

Notes: _____

_____

7. What is an artificial (derived) primary key? When should an artificial (or derived) primary key be used?

Skill Level: Intermediate

Expected answer:

> A derived key comes from a sequence. Usually, it is used when a concatenated key becomes too cumbersome to use as a foreign key.

Score: _____

Notes: _____

_____

8. When should you consider denormalization?

Skill Level: Intermediate

Expected answer:

Whenever performance analysis indicates it would be beneficial to do so without compromising data integrity.

Score: _____

Notes: _____

_____

Section average score: _____

Skill Level: _____

C Programming Questions

1. Explain the use of the compiler directive `#include` ?

   Skill Level: low

   Expected answer:

   > `#include` instructs the compiler to insert the contents of a file.

   Score: _____

   Notes: _____

   _____

2. Explain the use of the compiler directive `#define` ?

   Skill Level: low

   Expected answer:

   > It is used to set known values for the compiler. You can use it to state a known value's name for example: `#define DEBUG` or to state a substituted value for example: `#define NEWVALUE 8`.

   Score: _____

   Notes: _____

   _____

3. Explain the use of the compiler directive `#pragma` ?

   Skill Level: medium

   Expected answer:

   > `#pragma` alerts the compiler that the following instructions are to be ignored if the compiler does not understand them.

4. What directive is used to designate the end of a **#if** block of code?

Skill Level: low

Expected answer:

```
#endif
```

Score: _____

Notes: _____

_____

5. What markers are used to define comments within C code?

Skill Level: low

Expected answer:

/* and */

Score: _____

Notes: _____

_____

6. What symbols can be used in an identifier?

Skill Level: low

Expected answer:

Only the underscore can be used in the name of an identifier.

Score: _____

Notes: _____

_____

7. What symbol goes at the end of each C statement?

   Skill Level: low

   Expected answer:

   A semicolon goes at the end of each C statement.

   Score: _____

   Notes: _____

   _____

8. Describe a block.

   Skill Level: low

   Expected answer:

   A block is a series of C statements which are contained within a pair of curly braces.

   Score: _____

   Notes: _____

   _____

9. Can a C structure include a pointer to itself?

   Skill Level: low

   Expected answer:

   Yes

Score: _____

Notes: _____

_____

10. Is void main() the correct declaration for main()?

Skill Level: low

Expected answer:

No

Score: _____

Notes: _____

_____

11. What is the name of the function that every C program must contain and is the starting point for execution of your C program? How many times must it appear?

Skill level: Intermediate

Expected answer:

main()
It can appear only once.

Score: _____

Notes: _____

_____

12. What are the three techniques to define a constant variable in C?

Skill level: High

Expected answer:

Using the preprocessor directive `#define`:

For example:
```
#define pi 3.1415
```

Using the `const` keyword when defining the variable:

For example:
```
const float pi = 3.1415;
```

The third technique is to use an enumeration. An enumeration is used to define a set of constants. This is a useful technique to define a set of constants as opposed to using multiple #define preprocessor directives.

For example:

```
enum days {
    Monday=1
  , Tuesday
  , Wednesday
  , Thursday
  , Friday
  , Saturday
  , Sunday
};
```

Score: _____

Notes: _____

_____

13. What is a function prototype?

Skill level: Intermediate

Expected answer:

A function prototype is used to declare a function before it is actually used. It is considered good programming practice to declare all functions before their use. A function prototype declares the function name, its parameters, and its return type to the rest of the program prior to the function's actual declaration.

Score: _____

Notes: _____

_____

14. What is the name of the C library that contains standard I/O functions and how would you include it in a C program?

Skill level: Intermediate

Expected answer:

The name of the C library that contains standard I/O functions is **stdio.h**. Here is an example of how to include this in a C program:

```
...
#include <stdio.h>
...
```

Score: _____

Notes: _____

_____

15. Consider the code segment below. Why does this code print out that the values are equal? What would you do to correct this program?

```
1:   #include <stdio.h>
2:
3:   main() {
4:
5:      int a=5;
6:      int b=8;
7:
8:      if (a=b) {
9:         printf("The two values are equal.\n");
10:     } else {
11:        printf("The two values are NOT equal.\n");
12:     }
13:
14: }

% a.out
The two values are equal.
```

Skill level: Low

Expected answer:

The C programming language uses the == operator for checking equality. In our example, we accidentally used the = operator in line 8, which is used to assign a value. To correct the program, we would replace line 8 with the following

```
8: if (a == b) {
```

Score: _____

Notes: _____

_____

16. Write a simple code segment that declares a five element integer array named "a". After creating the array, continue the code segment by assigning an integer value to each of the 5 elements in the array. Finish off the example by looping through the array and printing each element to STDOUT using a FOR loop.

Skill level: Intermediate

Expected answer:

Here is an example code segment:

```
#include <stdio.h>

main() {

  int a[5];
  int i;

  a[0] = 10;
  a[1] = 20;
  a[2] = 30;
  a[3] = 40;
  a[4] = 50;

  for (i=0; i<5; i++) {
    printf("Element [%d] = %d\n", i, a[i]);
  }

}


% a.out
Element [0] = 10
Element [1] = 20
Element [2] = 30
Element [3] = 40
Element [4] = 50
```

Score: _____

Notes: _____

_____

17. What type of variable in C is used to store a memory address that can be used to point to another variable?

Skill level: Intermediate

Expected answer:

A *pointer* variable.

Score: _____

Notes: _____

_____

18. Write a sample code segment that declares two variables: (1) A normal integer variable named i that is assigned the value of 5 and (2) An a pointer to an integer variable named j. After declaring the two variables, assign the memory address of the variable i to j. Finally, print the value being pointed to by the variable j to standard out.

Skill level: High

Expected answer:

Score: _____

Notes: _____

_____

_____

19. Is there a problem with the code segment below? If so, how would you fix it?

```c
#include <stdio.h>

main() {

    int i=5;
    int *j;

    j = &i;

    printf("The value pointed to by j is %d.\n", *j);

}


% a.out
The value pointed to by j is 5.
```

Skill level: High

Expected answer:

The code segment above contains a common bug and will often cause a *segmentation fault* (core dump) when run. This is caused by attempting to use an un-initialized pointer variable. To fix this program, we should initialize the pointer variable p as in the following code:

```
#include <stdio.h>

main() {

  int *p;
  p = (int *) malloc(1*sizeof(int));  /* Initialize
Pointer */
  *p = 5;

  printf("The value pointed to by p is %d.\n", *p);

}
```

Score: _____

Notes: _____

_____

20. Why is it important to check the return value from a call to the *malloc()* function?

Skill level: Intermediate

Expected answer:

You should always check the return value of any call to the *malloc()* function as the return value can be used to determine if `malloc()` was actually able to allocate the requested memory from the heap. If the *malloc()* function returns a value of zero, this indicates that the *malloc()* function was not able to allocate the requested amount of memory - more than likely because the machine is out of memory.

Score: _____

Notes: _____

_____

21. Explain how Typedef names are automatically created for structure tags?

Skill Level: Intermediate

Expected answer:

They aren't automatically created.

Score: _____

Notes: _____

_____

22. What would you be doing to a file if you used the function *mmap()* and then used the function *sizeof()*?

Skill level: Intermediate

Expected answer:

Attempting to learn the size of the file before reading it in.

Score: _____

Notes: _____

_____

Section average score: _____

Skill Level: _____

C ++ Questions

1. Explain why you might need to use Language-Adaptable Header Files in a C++ program.

   Skill Level: low

   Expected answer:

   > C++ programs will often need to interface with C programs so it is important for the header file to be compatible with the C standards.

   Score: _____

   Notes: _____

   _____

2. Explain the significance of using Idempotent Header Files?

   Skill Level: low

   Expected answer:

   > An idempotent header file is one that works with multiple inclusions. An effective header file needs to be capable of adapting to different versions of C and C++.

   Score: _____

   Notes: _____

   _____

3. Which kind of comment automatically ends at the end of a line?

   Skill Level: low

   Expected answer:

A comment that is marked with a double slash (//) terminates at the end of a line.

Score: _____

Notes: _____

_____

4. Explain what is required to end a comment that originates with a slash and a star (/*)?

Skill Level: low

Expected answer:

A slash star comment will continue from line to line unless you insert a star slash (*/) to signal the end of the comment.

Score: _____

Notes: _____

_____

5. Is C++ case sensitive?

Skill Level: low

Expected answer:

Yes

Score: _____

Notes: _____

_____

6. Explain the significance of whitespace in C++ statements?

Skill Level: low

Expected answer:

Whitespace within statements is usually ignored. However, it can be used to make statements easier to read.

Score: _____

Notes: _____

_____

7. What is an expression?

Skill Level: low

Expected answer:

In C++ an expression is a statement that returns a value. For example 4+5; provides the value 9 making it an expression.

Score: _____

Notes: _____

_____

8. Explain why constants are always l-values?

Skill Level: low

Expected answer:

They aren't! Constants are r-values which means they reside on the right side of an assignment operator.

Score: _____

Notes: _____

_____

9. What is an assignment operator?

Skill Level: low

Expected answer:

The equal sign (=) is an assignment operator which causes the operand on the left side to have it's value changed to the value that is displayed on the right side.

Score: _____

Notes: _____

_____

10. Explain why constants are considered r-values?

Skill Level: low

Expected answer:

Constants are considered r-values because they reside on the right side of an assignment operator.

Score: _____

Notes: _____

_____

11. Explain the modulus operator?

Skill Level: medium

Expected answer:

The modulus operator is the mathematical operator that is used to determine the remainder that is dropped after an integer division.

12. Why do you always include a semicolon after an *if* statement?

Skill Level: low

Expected answer:

You should never include a semicolon after an *if* statement as it will terminate the statement causing it to be ineffective.

13. Explain the result of the expression income += 1000?

Skill Level: low

Expected answer:

The result would be the value of income plus 1000 so assuming income equals 50,000 the result would be 51,000.

14. What is the increment operator? What does it do?

Skill Level: low

Expected answer:

The increment operator is plus plus (++) and it increases a variable's value by one.

Score: _____

Notes: _____

_____

15. What is the decrement operator? What does it do?

Skill Level: low

Expected answer:

The decrement operator is minus minus (--) and it decreases a variable's value by one.

Score: _____

Notes: _____

_____

16. Explain the two varieties of the increment and decrement operators? What do they do?

Skill Level: low

Expected answer:

- When the operator is placed before the variable name it falls in the prefix category and when it comes after the variable name it is of the postfix variety.

- When the operator is in the prefix position it is processed before the assignment, when in the postfix position it is processed after assignment.

17. What the result of the following statement?

```
a = 7 + 2 * 6;
```

Skill Level: low

Expected answer:

The answer would be 19 because the multiplication operation is performed before the addition.

18. In what order are nested parentheses read?

Skill Level: medium

Expected answer:

Nested parentheses are read from the inside out.

19. Can you name six relational operators?

Skill Level: low

Expected answer:

The six relational operators are equals (==), not equals (!=), greater than (>), less than (<),greater than or equal to (>=) and less than or equal to (<=).

Score: _____

Notes: _____

_____

20. Can you name three logical operators?

Skill Level: low

Expected answer:

The three logical operators are:

And &&
Or ||
Not   !

Score: _____

Notes: _____

_____

21. What is a C++ ternary operator ? Explain what it does.

Skill Level: medium

Expected answer:

The ternary operator (?:) is a conditional operator which processes three expressions and returns the appropriate value.

22. What is the difference between direct and indirect recursion?

Skill Level: medium

Expected answer:

Direct recursion is a function calling itself. It is indirect recursion when a function calls another function which in turn calls the first function.

23. What are C++ classes?

Skill Level: medium

Expected answer:

Classes are data types that you create including data members or variables of various types which are called objects. Classes also contain methods or member functions which are used to perform services and manipulate the member data.

24. What is a virtual copy constructor?

Skill Level: medium

Expected answer:

A virtual copy constructor is a copy constructor which has been called by a virtual method within a class.

Score: _____

Notes: _____

_____

Section average score: _____

Skill Level: _____

PHP Scripting Questions

1. Name the variable in the following PHP script and describe how the code is manipulating the variable:

```
1. <?php
2. $vocal = "you're hired!";
3. print ("Convince me you are the best person for the
   job and I will say $utterance");
4. print ("<p>");
5. $vocal = "you're fired!";
6. print ("If you screw up I'm going to say $utterance");
7. ?>
```

Level: Low

Expected answer:

The variable "vocal" is created and first set to the value "You're hired!" Then it is reset to the new value "You're fired!" When executed it will display the following two lines of text in the browser:

```
Convince me you are the best person for the job and I
will say you're hired!

If you screw up I'm going to say you're fired!
```

Score: _____

Notes: _____

_____

2. Explain how to use PHP scripting to create a <p> tag in HTML to insert a paragraph break between lines of output from a PHP script?

Level: Low

Expected answer:

```
print ("<p>");
```

Score: _____

Notes: _____

_____

3. How do you include quotation marks in the output from a print statement?

Level: Low

Expected answer:

```
print (" \"Please do it right\"" );
```

Score: _____

Notes: _____

_____

4. Compare the difference in the delivery of results when using the "Post" method or the "Get" method to move information from an HTML form to a PHP script.

Level: Intermediate

Expected answer:

The "post" method delivers the information from the form hidden in the background, and the "get" method delivers the results as part of the URL.

Example: http://rampant.cc/cart/log_in.php?UserID=sara&pswd=terrier&submit=Enter

Score: _____

Notes: _____

_____

5. Explain the use of the PHP `array()` function.

Level: Low

Expected answer:

The `array()` function is used to create a variable to which you assign multiple values.

Score: _____

Notes: _____

_____

6. Give an example using the `array()` function to create and assign values to a simple array.

Level: Intermediate

Expected answer:

```
$girls = array ( "Amy", "Penny", "Linda", "Cindy" );
```

In other words:

```
variable = array ("value", "value", "value", "value" );
```

Score: _____

Notes: _____

_____

7. List the key numbers used to identify the individual values within the array you described in the answer to question # 6.

Level: Intermediate

Expected answer:

```
$girls[0] = "Amy";
$girls[1] = "Penny";
$girls[2] = "Linda";
$girls[3] = "Cindy";
```

Score: _____

Notes: _____

_____

8. Name the two sets of PHP tags that are always available to designate blocks of code within HTML.

Level: Low

Expected answer:

```
Standard     <?php   ?>
Script       <SCRIPT LANGUAGE="php"></SCRIPT>
```

Score: _____

Notes: _____

_____

9. List the standard data types that are available for use within PHP.

Level: Intermediate

Expected answer:

Integer, Double, Array, Boolean, String and Object

Score: _____

Notes: _____

_____

10. How do you declare variables in PHP?

Level: Low

Expected answer:

Variables are not declared in PHP, instead they are prefixed with a $ sign.

Score: _____

Notes: _____

_____

11. Describe the use of the dot (.) operator.

Level: Low

Expected answer:

The dot (.) operator is used to produce string concatenation in PHP.

Score: _____

Notes: _____

_____

12. Explain the use of Counted Loops.

Level: Intermediate

Expected answer:

You would use counted loops when you want to execute a statement or a list of statements for a predetermined number of repetitions. Do not add a semicolon to the end of the for statement. The block of code will be executed only once if a semicolon is added to the end of the for statement.

Score: _____

Notes: _____

_____

13. List and describe eight (8) type specifiers.

Level: Intermediate

Expected answer:

X	Display an integer as an uppercase hexadecimal number (base 16)
x	Display an integer as a lowercase hexadecimal number (base 16)
d	Display an argument as a decimal number
c	Display an integer as an ASCII equivalent
b	Display an integer as a binary number
o	Display an integer as an octal number (base 8)
f	Display an integer as a floating-point number (double)
s	Display an argument as a string

Score: _____

Notes: _____

_____

14. Explain the use of the n12br() function.

Level: Intermediate

Expected answer:

The n12br() function inserts line breaks into the web page by turning every new line into a break so as to prevent the text from running together in an awkward lump.

Score: _____

Notes: _____

_____

15. Describe the integer returned by the time () function?

Level: Intermediate

Expected answer:

It is a timestamp, the number of seconds that have elapsed since the UNIX epoch which was midnight GMT on January 1, 1970.

Score: _____

Notes: _____

_____

16. Explain the $_POST superglobal?

Level: Intermediate

Expected answer:

It is a built in associative array that holds the values that have been submitted as part of a POST request.

Score: _____

Notes: _____

_____

17. What is a cookie?

Level: Low

Expected answer:

A cookie is a file containing a minimal amount of data that is stored by a web browser in response to a request from a script or a server. They are often used as a means to identify and track web site visitors.

Score: _____

Notes: _____

_____

Section average score: _____

Skill Level: _____

Non-Technical Questions

When conducting an on-site or telephone interview, it's very important that you be able to assess non-technical information about your job candidate. These non-technical factors include motivation, thinking skills, and personal attitude. All of these factors have a direct bearing on the ultimate success of the candidate in your shop. They also give you an idea about the potential longevity of a particular candidate.

Each of these questions is deliberately ambiguous and probing so that the job candidate will have an opportunity to speak freely. Often these questions will give you a very good idea of the suitability of the candidate for the position. Remember, in many IT shops technical ability is secondary to the ability of the candidate to function as a team member within the organization.

1. What are your plans if you don't get this job?

    Answer: _____

    Comment: _____

    _____

    This question can reveal a great deal about the motivation of the job candidate. If the candidate indicates that he/she will change career fields, going into an unrelated position, then this person may not have a long-term motivation to stay within the IT industry. If, on the other hand, the candidate responds that he will continue to pursue opportunities within the specific technical area, then the candidate is probably dedicated to the job for which he is being interviewed.

2. How do you feel about overtime?

Answer: _____

Comment: _____

_____

This is an especially loaded question, because any honest job candidate is going to tell you that they don't like to work overtime. As we know, the reality of today's IT world is that the professional will occasionally have to work evenings and weekends. This question is essential if you're interviewing for a position that requires non-traditional hours, such as a network administrator or database administrator, where the bulk of the production changes will occur on evenings, weekends, and holidays.

3. Describe your biggest non-technical flaw.

Answer: _____

Comment: _____

_____

This question provides insight into the personality of the job candidate, as well as their honesty and candor. Responses are unpredictable and may range from "I don't suffer fools gladly" to "I have difficulty thinking after I've been on the job for 16 hours". Again, there is no right or wrong answer to this question, but it may indicate how well the candidate is going to function during critical moments. More importantly, this question gives an idea of the level of self-awareness of the candidate and gauges whether or not they are actively working to improve their non-technical skills.

3. Describe your least favorite boss or professor.

Answer: _____

Comment: _____

_____

The answer to this question will reveal the candidate's opinions and attitudes about being supervised by others. While there is no correct response to this question, it can shed a great deal of light on the candidate's interpersonal skills.

4. Where do you plan to be ten years from now?

Answer: _____

Comment: _____

_____

This is an especially important question for the IT job candidate because it reveals a lot about their motivations. As we know, the IT job industry does not have a lot of room for advancement within the technical arena, and someone who plans to rise within the IT organization will be required to move into management at some point. It's interesting that the response to this question is often made to be overly important, especially amongst those managers that hear the response "in ten years I would like to have your job."

5. How important is money to you?

Answer: _____

Comment: _____

_____

Again, this is an extremely misleading question, because even though many IT professionals deeply enjoy their jobs, and some would even do it for free, money is a primary motivator for people in the workplace. This question provides an easy opportunity to find out whether or not your candidate is being honest with you.

An appropriate answer for the candidate might be to say that he greatly enjoys his work within IT but that he needs to be able to maintain some level of income in order to support his family. A bonus benefit of this question is it also provides insight into the demographic structure of the job candidate, namely their marital status, as well as the age of their children, and whether or not they have immediate family in the area. It is well known within the IT industry that job candidates are most likely to remain with the company if they have a large extended family group within the immediate area

6. Why did you leave your last job?

Answer: _____

Comment: _____

_____

This is one of the most loaded questions of all, and one that can be extremely revealing about the personality of the IT job candidate. The most appropriate answer to this question is that the previous job was not technically challenging enough, or that the candidate was bored.

However, periodically you will find job candidates who will express negativity regarding the work environment, the quality of the management, and the personalities of the co-workers. This of course, should be a major red flag because it may indicate that this job candidate does not possess the interpersonal skills required to succeed in a team environment.

7. If you were a vegetable, what vegetable would you be?

Answer: _____

Comment: _____

_____

On its face, this is a totally ludicrous and ambiguous question, but it gives you an opportunity to assess the creative thinking skills of the job candidate. For example, if the job candidate merely replies "I don't know", he may not possess the necessary creative thinking skills required for a systems analyst or developer position.

A creative candidate will simply pick a vegetable, and describe in detail why that particular vegetable suits their personality. For example, the job candidate might say "I would be broccoli because I am health-oriented, have a bushy head, and go well with Chinese food."

8. Describe the month of June.

Answer: _____

Comment: _____

_____

The answer to this question also provides insight into the thinking ability of the job candidate. For example, most job candidates may reply that June is a summer month, with longer days, hot weather, and an ideal vacation time. The candidate with an engineering or scientific point of view might reply instead that June is a month with 30 days that immediately precedes the summer equinox.

9. Why do you want to work here?

    Answer: _____

    Comment: _____

    _____

This is the candidate's opportunity to express why he might be a good fit for your particular organization. It also indicates whether the candidate has taken the time to research the company and the work environment. Is the candidate applying for this position solely because he needs a job, any job, or because he has specifically singled out your company due to some appealing characteristic of the work environment?

This question can also add information about the motivation of the job candidate, because a job candidate who is highly motivated to work for a particular firm will make the effort to research the company, the work environment, and even the backgrounds of individual managers.

Using a powerful search engine such as Google, the savvy IT candidate can quickly glean information about the person who is interviewing them. Having detailed knowledge of the organization is a very positive indicator that the candidate has given a lot of thought to the particular position and is evidence of high motivation.

10. What do you know about our company?

Answer: _____

Comment: _____

_____

If the prospective employee has little or no knowledge about the company, then he will also have little idea about how he can benefit the company. A candidate who has not gone to the trouble of researching the organization may be after a job, any job.

A candidate who has taken the time to explore the company will probably have specific ideas in mind about what he can bring to the organization. The initiative required by the candidate to research the company is a good sign that he is proactive and not passive dead weight.

If the candidate has some knowledge of the company's mission and function, this will also become apparent in the questions he asks you. He will already be thinking about how he can fit in and how his skills can be utilized. These are desirable traits of a problem-solver.

11. Why do you want to work for this company? Why should we hire you?

Answer: _____

Comment: _____

_____

The answer to this question can reveal whether the candidate is merely shopping for a job or has true interest in the company and the position. It is important that the candidate show some passion for the field. If he does not, he will probably never be creative in the work environment and he will not represent a solution for you.

Does the candidate have a core belief that his particular set of skills can benefit you? Answers such as "I believe my experience can make a difference here," or "I believe your company will provide an environment that more directly engages my interest," or "Working for your company will provide challenges that excite me" are good starters.

12. Why are you looking for a new job?

     Answer: _____

     Comment: _____

     _____

Typical reasons for seeking a new job include the desire to advance in the field and boredom in a job that offers few fresh challenges. These are positive motivations, but there can be negative ones as well. There may be personal conflicts between the candidate and other team members or management that have become so adversarial that the candidate is compelled to leave.

While not necessarily eliminating a candidate from consideration, personal friction in the previous job does raise a red flag. It may be that the candidate is an unfortunate victim of backroom politics. However, if he confides in you regarding the shortcomings of his supervisors or fellow employees while taking no responsibility himself, consider yourself warned.

13. Tell us about yourself or your background.

Answer: _____

Comment: _____

_____

This is probably asked more than any other question in interviews. It is the main opportunity for the candidate to describe his experiences, motivations, and vision of himself as it relates to the company.

The candidate should provide clear examples of how his abilities were used in the past to solve problems. If the candidate just repeats the information in the résumé, he is probably only going through the motions and has no clear vision of his role in the company.

Even worse, if the candidate contradicts the résumé, there is evidence of a serious problem.

14. What are three major characteristics that you bring to the job?

Answer: _____

Comment: _____

_____

The candidate should offer specific skills or traits that he believes will be useful in the position. If the candidate is unable to relate these characteristics to the job, he has obviously not thought much about his role in the organization. You are interested in finding someone who has ideas about how he can hit the ground running and make a real difference to the company.

15. Describe the "ideal" job... the "ideal" supervisor.

Answer: _____

Comment: _____

_____

This question is not as open-ended as it may seem. If the candidate's ideal job has little or nothing in common with the position he is interviewing for, he is unlikely to be a good fit. The candidate's response should match fairly well with the requirements of the position.

The candidate's description of the ideal supervisor can provide clues about how well the candidate works with superiors. Beware the candidate who seizes this as an opportunity to denigrate past managers.

16. How would you handle a tough customer?

Answer: _____

Comment: _____

_____

Can the candidate provide examples of instances when difficult clients were won over? An effective communicator can strike a balance between meeting the needs of the customer and dealing with unrealistic expectations.

Above all, the candidate should indicate that he understands the necessity of "going the extra mile" to alleviate the concerns of the customer. Providing service to the client or end user is fundamental to the success of any enterprise.

17. How would you handle working with a difficult co-worker?

Answer: _____

Comment: _____

_____

This is similar to the last question. The candidate should relate an example of a conflict with a co-worker or team member that was successfully resolved. What you are looking for is evidence that the candidate is able to facilitate communication and lead a difficult project to a successful conclusion.

18. When would you be available to start if you were selected?

Answer: _____

Comment: _____

_____

19. How does this position match your career goals?

Answer: _____

Comment: _____

_____

This is an excellent question to ascertain whether the candidate truly sees the position as an integral part of his career path. Does the candidate believe the knowledge and experience he will gain from this job will move him to where he wants to be?

A thorough answer to this question will lead into the next one.

20. What are your career goals (a) 3 years from now; (b) 10 years from now?

Answer: _____

Comment: _____

_____

The answer to this question will indicate the level of commitment the candidate feels towards the job and the company. If the candidate has a goal in mind, how well does it fit with the job he is applying for?

When the candidate describes his goals, does he speak in terms of the skills and abilities he hopes to acquire that will prepare him for his eventual role, or does he simply want to be the CEO, with little thought of what it might take to get there?

The interviewer may be surprised by how often the candidate will talk about goals that are unrelated to the position.

21. What do you like to do in your spare time?

Answer: _____

Comment: _____

_____

This question provides an opportunity to learn more about the character of the candidate, and to judge whether his outside interests complement his professional life. Is the candidate well-rounded or one-dimensional? Does he tend to sustain an interest over time?

22. What motivates you to do a good job?

Answer: _____

Comment: _____

_____

If the candidate responds "making money" or "avoiding the wrath of my boss," you may have a problem. The candidate should describe some positive motivation, such as a new challenge, and tie it to a specific example of a time in the past when the motivation reaped personal rewards and results on the job.

23. What two or three things are most important to you at work?

Answer: _____

Comment: _____

_____

The answer to this can reveal much about how the candidate sees himself on the job. Does the candidate mention things such as the importance of interpersonal communication, or responding quickly to crisis situations, things that facilitate job performance, or does he seem to be more worried about the timeliness of his coffee breaks?

24. What qualities do you think are essential to be successful in this kind of work?

Answer: _____

Comment: _____

_____

Does the candidate have a realistic idea of what the work environment requires of him, and do the qualities of the candidate match the job? Does the candidate have an example of a past job experience when these qualities were called upon with beneficial results?

25. How does your previous work experience prepare you for this position?

Answer: _____

Comment: _____

_____

This question is related to many of the others. If the candidate is able to articulate a clear idea of how his previous experience and training has prepared him for the responsibilities of the new position, he will be well ahead of many other interviewees.

26. How do you define "success?"

Answer: _____

Comment: _____

_____

If the answer doesn't fit the position, the candidate may be unhappy in the field or quickly become bored. This indicates that the candidate may not be committed to staying with the company for very long.

27. What has been your most significant accomplishment to date?

Answer: _____

Comment: _____

_____

The candidate should be able to relate a specific example of an achievement that demonstrates a desirable quality for the job. The candidate should focus on action and results, rather than long-winded descriptions of situations.

The answer to this question can provide insight into situations that the candidate may handle especially well. The candidate should demonstrate an ability to persevere and overcome obstacles. Did the person deliver more than was expected of him in a difficult situation?

28. Describe a failure and how you dealt with it.

Answer: _____

Comment: _____

_____

This type of negative question can be extremely revealing. It can indicate significant weaknesses or problems that may interfere with the ability to do the job.

Was the failure a catastrophic one, or a relatively minor problem? Was the candidate able to learn from the experience and apply the knowledge to future situations?

The answer to this question can also reveal how much personal accountability and responsibility the candidate accepts. If the candidate blames the failure on others, he is not likely to learn from his mistakes.

As with most interview questions, this questions is designed to provide insight into the overall personality of the candidate, giving you a fuller appreciation of the strengths, as well as the weaknesses, of the person.

29. What leadership roles have you held?

Answer: _____

Comment: _____

_____

This answer should indicate not only that the candidate has the leadership experience to succeed in the new job, but that he has the ability to work well with others and is able to shoulder the responsibility and deal with the pressure associated with the requirements of the position.

30. Are you willing to travel?

Answer: _____

Comment: _____

_____

The answer here will demonstrate how committed to the company the candidate is likely to be. If the candidate dismisses the idea of travel completely, he may lack the motivation you are looking for.

31. What have you done in the past year to improve yourself?

Answer: _____

Comment: _____

_____

This question can shed more light on the personality of the candidate. If the candidate has been motivated by the goal of obtaining this position, he will be able to demonstrate that he has taken the initiative to prepare himself for it.

If the candidate instead chooses to describe the benefits of his basket-weaving class, he may indeed be the better for it, but it has little relevance to solving the problems he would soon encounter in the new position.

32. In what areas do you feel you need further education and training to be successful?

Answer: _____

Comment: _____

_____

If the answer has nothing to do with the offered position, the candidate may soon become bored. This question is similar to others and should dovetail with other answers about goals and career path.

33. What are your salary requirements?

Answer: _____

Comment: _____

_____

If the candidate mentions a figure that is too low, he may be uninformed or desperate. On the other hand, if his financial expectations are unreasonable, he should probably be eliminated from consideration.

Policies, Processes and Procedures

The following questions are designed to zero in on key aspects of the candidate's personality and ability to perform. You may find it helpful to assign each response a score between 1 and 5 (a shorthand assessment technique that may also be used with many of the preceding questions).

You are trying to gauge the candidate's ability to act in accordance with established guidelines, follow standard procedures in crisis situations, communicate and enforce organizational policies and procedures, and recognize and constructively conform to unwritten rules or practices.

1. On some jobs it is necessary to act strictly in accordance with policy. Give me an example when you were expected to act in accordance with policy even when it was not convenient. What did you do?

    Expected answer: Did the candidate follow policy because of commitment to it, even if a reason could be given for breaking it? Was there non-conformity to policy because of personal style, disrespect for those who made the policy, or revenge/dishonesty?

    Score: _____

    Comment: _____

    _____

2. What types of experience have you had in managing situations that involve potentially high money loss situations to ensure your job effectiveness?

    Expected answer: Did the candidate have a "no exceptions" strategy which showed systematic and rigorous use of policy and procedures to ensure consistency? Was there a dislike for rules and preferences to ensure consistency? Was there dislike for rules and preference for doing the job his/her own way?

    Score: _____

    Comment: _____

    _____

3. Describe a time when you found a policy or procedure challenging or difficult to adhere to. How did you handle it

Expected answer: Did the candidate take great pains to adhere to the policy and communicate the difficulty to proper management for review/revision? Was there an unnecessary risky deviation from policy, and no communication of either the challenge or deviation to management?

Score: _____

Comment: _____

_____

Quality

The traits of a candidate who does quality work include their ability to maintain high standards despite pressing deadlines, establish high standards and measures, do work right the first time, inspect material for flaws, test new methods thoroughly, and reinforce excellence as a fundamental priority.

1. Describe a situation in which a crucial deadline was nearing, but you didn't want to compromise quality. How did you deal with it?

Expected answer: Did the candidate maintain high quality through investing additional resources, moving deadlines, or making a statement of work in progress? Was there a quality sacrifice, possibly resulting in additional problems at a later time?

Score: _____

Comment: _____

_____

2. Describe something you developed or coordinated that had to be exactly right. Exactly how did you test it?

   Expected answer: Did the candidate rigorously identify potential sources of problems, systematically address them, and run ample trails? Was there a brief accounting for possible problems, insufficient experimentation, or minimal piloting?

   Score: _____

   Comment: _____

   _____

3. Describe an effort you undertook to make product/service quality a fundamental priority in your business. Exactly what steps did you take to do this?

   Expected answer: Did the candidate implement training and error prevention/control/correction systems, or apply other systematic approaches? Was there a haphazard or inadequate support of quality functions?

   Score: _____

   Comment: _____

   _____

Commitment to Task

Commitment to task involves the ability to take responsibility for actions and outcomes and persist despite obstacles. To be available around the clock in case of emergency, give long hours to the job, demonstrate dependability in difficult circumstances, and show a sense of urgency about getting the job done.

1. Describe a difficult situation in which you took full responsibility for actions and outcomes. How did you act on this?

   Expected answer: Did the candidate publicly claim responsibility, and then carefully manage this situation to success, possibly one involving other parties with divergent goals? Was there allowance of others to accept blame, and little effort to resolve a difficult situation?

   Score: _____

   Comment: _____

   _____

2. Some people can be counted on to go the extra mile when their organization really needs it. Describe a time when you demonstrated dependability in trying circumstances.

   Expected answer: Did the candidate work long hours or perform unusual job duties to help the organization get through a personnel shortage, etc.? Was there minimal extra effort, consistent with the notion that it was the company's problem?

   Score: _____

   Comment: _____

   _____

3. Describe a time when you gave long hours to the job. For example, tell me about when you took work home, worked on weekends, or maintained long hours due to system maintenance.

   Expected answer: Did the candidate show self-direction and initiative in working particularly long hours, with clear dedication to a meaningful objective? Was there compliance to routine work requirements, possibly with resentment about what was expected?

Score: _____

Comment: _____

_____

4. Give me an example of a time when you demonstrated a sense of urgency about getting results.

    Expected answer: Did the candidate take immediate action directed toward a specific objective, so that non-task activities and interests were given low priority while productivity and efficiency were of prime importance? Was there little emphasis on effectiveness/speed/efficiency?

Score: _____

Comment: _____

_____

Planning, Prioritizing and Goal Setting

Your network administrator may be called upon to wear many different hats in this position. He/She should have the ability to prepare for emerging customer needs, manage multiple projects, and determine project urgency in a meaningful and practical way. Other desirable abilities include the ability to use goals to guide actions and create detailed action plans and the ability to organize and schedule people and tasks.

1. Describe a situation that illustrates how well you manage multiple projects simultaneously.

    Expected answer: Did the candidate keep all projects moving on a pace to hit deadlines and in a manageable, systematic, quality way, and using a meaningful approach to prioritizing? Was there haphazard allotment of resources to different tasks, with unproductive and unnecessary chaos?

Score: _____

Comment: _____

_____

2. Priorities can be set meaningfully based on ease of task, customer size, deadlines, or a number of other factors. Describe a time when it was challenging for you to prioritize.

Expected answer: Did the candidate use a sensible set or priorities and apply it consistently? Was there excess bouncing of resources, resulting in inefficiency, or a poor choice of criteria on which to prioritize?

Score: _____

Comment: _____

_____

3. Think of a project in which you skillfully coordinated people, tasks, and schedules. How did you do it?

Expected answer: Did the candidate use a systematic approach to identify tasks, people who can do the tasks, schedules, and constraints? Was there a simplistic approach that was inadequate given the complexities of the project?

Score: _____

Comment: _____

_____

Attention to Detail

Attention to detail involves the ability to be alert in a high-risk environment, the ability to follow detailed procedures and ensure accuracy in documentation and data. Your network administrator may be called upon to carefully monitor gauges, instruments, or processes. He/She should be able to concentrate on routine work details and organize and maintain a system of records.

1. Describe a time when you had to apply changes to a mission critical system. What did you do to insure the stability of the system? What actions did you take and what were the results?

   Expected answer: Did the candidate dutifully monitor all potentially troublesome aspects of the environment, and address anything that seemed imperfect. Was there a casual awareness of potential trouble spots, and reliance on subsequent quick reactions rather than prevention?

   Score: _____

   Comment: _____

   _____

2. Select an experience from you past, which illustrates your ability to be attentive to detail when monitoring the systems environment. Tell me, in detail, what happened.

   Expected answer: Did the candidate show commitment to monitoring and understanding equipment and to using a strategy to ensure/enhance attention to detail? Was there little awareness of potential distractions, over-dependence on technology, or overconfidence?

   Score: _____

   Comment: _____

   _____

3. How have you gone about ensuring accuracy and consistency in a document or data you were preparing? Tell me about a specific case in which your attention to detail paid off.

   Expected answer: Did the candidate take clear precautions such as proofing thoroughly, double-checking, verifying format consistency, etc.? Was there only a cursory spot check?

   Score: _____

   Comment: _____

   _____

4. Tell me about your experience in dealing with routine work. What kinds of problems did you have to overcome in order to concentrate on the details of the job?

   Expected answer: Did the candidate use a strategy to maintain attentiveness during routine work? Was there acceptance of diminished alertness, with little effort being made to remove/reduce it?

   Score: _____

   Comment: _____

   _____

5. Give me an example that demonstrates your ability to organize and maintain a system of records.

   Expected answer: Did the candidate initiate or show commitment to a systematic method for organization or record keeping? Was there ineffective record keeping, overconfidence in memory, or dependence on others?

Score: _____

Comment: _____

_____

Initiative

Initiative includes the ability to bring about great results from ordinary circumstances, prepare for problems or opportunities in advance, transform leads into productive business outcomes, undertake additional responsibilities, and respond to situations as they arise without supervision.

1. Tell me about a situation in which you aggressively capitalized on an opportunity and converted something ordinary into something special

   Expected answer: Did the candidate put a unique twist on a routine situation to yield unusually positive results, probably not achieved by others in similar situations? Was there an accomplishment of little magnitude or that should have been expected of anyone in that situation?

   Score: _____

   Comment: _____

   _____

2. Describe something you've done that shows how you can respond to situations as they arise without supervision.

   Expected answer: Did the candidate take reasonable and quick action with an appropriate amount of information or research, warranting the independence? Was there use of authority inappropriately, excess procrastination, or a bad decision?

Score: _____

Comment: _____

_____

3. Describe a time when you voluntarily undertook a special project above and beyond your normal responsibilities.

   Expected answer: Did the candidate volunteer for a large task/responsibility despite an already full workload and succeed without undue compromise of other responsibilities? Was there an insignificant, short-term addition, or an unnecessary sacrifice of other areas?

   Score: _____

   Comment: _____

   _____

4. Many people have good ideas, but few act on them. Tell me how you've transformed a good idea into a productive business outcome.

   Expected answer: Did the candidate generate a meaningful action plan to bring the idea to reality? Was there a haphazard, unrealistic, or unproductive transformation?

   Score: _____

   Comment: _____

   _____

Index

J

L

M

N

O

About Janet Burleson

As a top executive with BEI., Janet Burleson has extensive experience recruiting, hiring and managing Information Technology professionals.

As an expert Web design consultant Janet provides high level web consulting services that improve the market status of Fortune 500 companies including web search rank positioning, keyword optimization, web content optimization, web community relationships, web site design, web usage tracking and web site configuration.

Janet is also one of the world's pioneering horse trainers, having developed the successful Guide Horse Foundation donating her time and effort to train miniature horses to guide the blind. www.guidehorse.com

About Mike Reed

When he first started drawing, Mike Reed drew just to amuse himself.

It wasn't long, though, before he knew he wanted to be an artist.

Today he does illustrations for children's books, for magazines, for catalogs, and for ads.

He also teaches illustration at the College of Visual Art in St. Paul, Minnesota. Mike Reed says, "Making pictures is like acting — you can paint yourself into the action." He often paints on the computer, but he also draws in pen and ink and paints in acrylics. He feels that learning to draw well is the key to being a successful artist.

Mike is regarded as one of the nation's premier illustrators and is the creator of the popular "Flame Warriors" illustrations at **www.flamewarriors.com**. A renowned children's artist, Mike has also provided the illustrations for dozens of children's books.

Mike Reed has always enjoyed reading. As a young child, he liked the Dr. Seuss books. Later, he started reading biographies and war stories. One reason why he feels lucky to be an illustrator is because he can listen to books on tape while he works. Mike is available to provide custom illustrations for all manner of publications at reasonable process. Mike can be reached at **www.mikereedillustration.com**.

The Oracle In-Focus Series

The *Oracle In-Focus* series is a unique publishing paradigm, targeted at Oracle professionals who need fast and accurate working examples of complex issues. *Oracle In-Focus* books are unique because they have a super-tight focus and quickly provide Oracle professionals with what they need to solve their problems.

Oracle In-Focus books are designed for the practicing Oracle professional. Oracle In-Focus books are an affordable way for all Oracle professionals to get the information they need, and get it fast.

Expert Authors – All *Oracle In-Focus* authors are content experts and are carefully screened for technical ability and communications skills.

Online Code Depot – All code scripts from *Oracle In-Focus* are available on the web for instant download. Those who purchase a book will get the URL and password to download their scripts.

Lots of working examples – *Oracle In-Focus* is packed with working examples and pragmatic tips.

No theory – Practicing Oracle professionals know the concepts, they need working code to get started fast.

Concise – All *Oracle In-Focus* books are less than 400 pages and get right to-the-point of the tough technical issues.

Tight focus - The *Oracle In-Focus* series addresses tight topics and targets specific technical areas of Oracle technology.

Affordable – Reasonably priced, *Oracle In-Focus* books are the perfect solution to challenging technical issues.

www.Rampant-Books.com

Free!
Oracle 10g Senior DBA Reference Poster

This 24 x 36 inch quick reference includes the important data columns and relationships between the DBA views, allowing you to quickly write complex data dictionary queries.

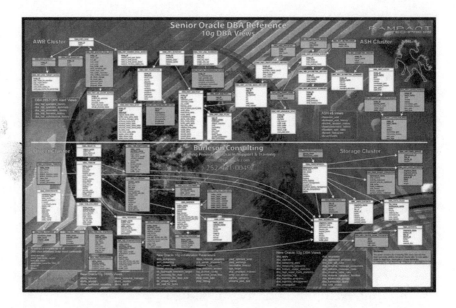

This comprehensive data dictionary reference contains the most important columns from the most important Oracle10g DBA views. Especially useful are the Automated Workload Repository (AWR) and Active Session History (ASH) DBA views.

WARNING - This poster is not suitable for beginners. It is designed for senior Oracle DBAs and requires knowledge of Oracle data dictionary internal structures. You can get your poster at this URL:

www.rampant.cc/poster.htm